Personalizing Learning

How to Transform Learning through System-Wide Reform

Phil Jones
and Maureen Burns

Published by
Network Continuum Education
PO Box 635, Stafford ST16 1BF

www.networkcontinuum.co.uk
www.continuumbooks.com

An imprint of The Continuum International Publishing Group Ltd

First published 2006
© Phil Jones and Maureen Burns 2006

ISBN-13: 978 1 85539 210 6
ISBN-10: 1 85539 210 0

The rights of Phil Jones and Maureen Burns to be identified as the authors of this work have been asserted in accordance with Sections 77 and 78 of the Copyright, Designs and Patents Act 1988.

All rights reserved. No part of this publication may be reproduced, stored in a retrieval system or reproduced or transmitted in any form or by any means, electronic, mechanical, photocopying, recording or otherwise, without the prior written permission of the publishers. This book may not be lent, resold, hired out or otherwise disposed of by the way of trade in any form of binding or cover other than that in which it is published, without the prior consent of the publishers.

Every effort has been made to contact the copyright holders of materials reproduced in this book. The publishers apologize for any omissions and will be pleased to rectify them at the earliest opportunity.

Managing editor: Lynn Bresler – Lynn Bresler Editorial Services
Layout: Marc Maynard – Network Continuum Education
Cover design: Marc Maynard – Network Continuum Education
Proofreader and indexer: Sue Lightfoot

Printed in Great Britain by MPG Books Ltd, Bodmin, Cornwall

Contents

1	The context for personalizing learning	5
2	The need for change: from incrementalism to transformation	11
3	Policy and action	23
4	School partnerships driving personalization	29
5	The power of data	37
6	Harnessing the strength of business and industry	43
7	Local authorities at the heart of personalization	49
8	Key expectations for the system components	53
	References and acknowledgements	55
	Index	57

Chapter 1

The context for personalizing learning

During the past two years an enormous amount of literature has been generated about the ideas around personalizing learning. There is widespread recognition that effective schools already offer a highly personalized curriculum. However, many schools are criticized for offering a one-size-fits-all experience. Current international comparisons point to inequity in pupil attainment in the English system of education. Much of this book is focused on examining that inequity and in promoting strategies that are intended to challenge and overcome the current links between disadvantage and low attainment. The government's figures for Key Stage 2 results in 2004 demonstrate that while 81 per cent of pupils nationally reached expected levels of attainment in English, the figure drops to only 58 per cent for those in receipt of free school meals.

Personalizing learning is not a specific policy or strategy – rather it is an overarching theme that was introduced by David Miliband as Minister for Standards in 2004. Miliband's expressed view was that, at the core of personalizing learning, 'every aspect of teaching and support is designed around a pupil's needs'. In our view personalizing learning is the process of tailoring or matching teaching and learning to meet individual needs, interests and aptitudes in order to enable every student to succeed within the education system.

The need to achieve this has never been more acute or urgent. Despite successive improvement strategies there remains a fundamental weakness in equality of opportunity based upon differences in socio-economic status. Those children from lower socio-economic groups continue to achieve far less well than their peers from more favoured backgrounds. Significant numbers of ethnic minority groups struggle to succeed in our schools and many students are not well disposed towards the process of learning. In addition, the world of business and industry persists in claiming that the school system fails to produce sufficient school leavers with appropriate skills and knowledge. This is at a time when fewer students pursue higher education and careers in science which, we are told, will have severe economic consequences for the nation.

Much of the debate about personalizing learning is focused on the extent to which teachers in schools are being successful in providing a range of experiences to meet the diverse needs of all students in their care. In this book we propose that this is necessary but insufficient. In order for teachers and schools to deliver a personalized experience, all other parts of the system need to agree and establish their own distinctive contribution to the personalization agenda and to be accountable for it. In other words, the government, the DfES and its partner agencies, together with local authorities and the world of business and industry, need to develop a greater clarity about the relationship between their current priorities and the creation of a personalized education system.

Of course, the attempt to organize the curriculum and teaching and learning in such a way that they are more carefully matched to the needs of learners is not new. Good schools and teachers have, over time, developed a range of strategies that have been more or less successful. Such strategies include resource-based learning, differentiation, modular curricula, vocational courses, mentoring and parental involvement, to mention but a few. The development of provision for children with special educational needs, gifted and talented children and for children for whom English is an additional language are also part of this rich picture. Good teachers and good schools have always striven to match need to provision.

Previous government policies, initiatives and programmes have also attempted to meet the challenge of differential provision and these have recently included:

- *Excellence in Cities*, which was introduced in September 1999 to secondary schools. The launch of EIC was one of the policy developments resulting from the 1997 White Paper *Excellence in Schools* which stated an intention to create 'inclusive schooling ...that recognises the different talents of all children and delivers excellence for all'. The policy was based on a major targeting of resources in deprived areas with the aim of transforming secondary urban education. Key focus areas for the policy are teaching and learning, behaviour, attendance and leadership. Early indicators suggest that this initiative is having some success in raising attainment and in particular for pupils in mathematics at the end of Key Stage 3.

- *Education Action Zones* were also established during the same period – part of the *Excellence in Cities* programme, this now involves over 130 Zones which are attempting to develop innovative solutions to education and to broker partnerships in deprived urban and rural areas.

- *Beacon Schools* – this initiative ran from 1998 to August 2005 and had the aim of transferring effective practice from high-performing schools to others. It met with limited success, often because of a lack of buy-in from the non-Beacon schools and from difficulties in generating the necessary capacity to share practice.

- *The Leadership Incentive Grant* – begun in 2003, this has involved over 1,400 schools in challenging circumstances and has encouraged schools to strengthen leadership and enhance teaching and learning through collaboration.

The focus for all of these programmes has been, to a greater or lesser extent, to improve education and raise standards for lower attaining students. The data available (see Chapter 2) indicates that whatever gains might have been made in individual schools or within the programmes, performance in secondary education across the country has changed little; and the tail of underperformance remains one of the worst in the developed world. Current provision is clearly still not meeting the needs of many learners.

So, a question that needs to be asked is in what ways can what has become known as the personalization of learning be qualitatively different from what has gone before, and how should the education system respond to it. More importantly, how can the response be qualitatively different from what has gone before and so play a part in transforming the learning landscape of the country.

This transformation will involve understanding how new and important knowledge about how children learn can be harnessed to techniques to understand and use the data we now have access to, that is, data on prior attainment, the impact of social and economic context, and gender, and what effect these and other factors have on educational success or failure. The use of these new areas of knowledge poses challenges to the education system to make them work effectively for the benefit of learners. At the very least, those of us who are parents need to be asking how this new knowledge is changing for the better what children are experiencing in our schools.

It is our contention that the only way in which the maximization of the potential of a personalized approach to learning can be achieved is through the effective collaboration of all the key players of the education system. This collaboration must have as its sole focus meeting the complex and diverse needs of learners. The system must become needs-led rather than provider-driven.

In this book we will explore how the different components which make up the education system can interact with new knowledge and methodologies to more effectively achieve this goal.

At the forefront of all this we need to remember that the purpose is to educate the whole child. The education system must be driven by finding the most effective ways to ensure that all children are served well by the system in becoming happy, well-motivated learners capable of making their own distinctive and productive contribution to society and to changing society for the better. Social cohesion and economic well-being cannot be realized when the system marginalizes significant numbers of learners and fails to get the best from many across the full range of the attainment spectrum. This is the challenge to the system which personalizing learning has to meet.

In this context, what do we mean by the education system? In essence, the system is the total of those elements that have a stake in and a significant contribution to make to the education of children.

The key components are:

- schools – including teachers and other school employees, governors and school partnerships
- local authorities
- the government and its agencies
- business and industry.

For each of these components we need to be clear about the professional expectations we have of them and the contributions they are expected to make. Over recent years there has been a significant increase in the levels of accountability placed on schools for ensuring that their efforts are fully focused on raising standards and motivating learners. This is evidenced through the publication of

- Ofsted reports
- performance tables
- attendance data.

To a large degree the professional expectations and public responsibilities of schools are clear, well articulated, generally understood and objectively assessed. There now needs to be a similar accountability framework placed on all other components of the system such as:

- all divisions of the DfES
- National College of School Leadership (NCSL)
- local authorities
- Training and Development Agency for Schools (TDA).

It is notoriously difficult to create an accountability framework for provider organizations which does more than measure inputs to the education system and the quality of the processes used to underpin such provision. Traditionally agencies such as NCSL or the TDA measure the success of their core business through offering quality services in headteacher training or initial teacher training. While their stated aims and purposes are to raise students' standards of achievement it is difficult to discern how this bears directly on the personalizing learning agenda. To date the deliverables of these organizations have largely been measured through rates of participation and engagement with the targeted client group. Arguably this is an approach which measures processes and to some extent some specific outputs. However, in future it is critical that work of this nature should take place within a shared framework for accountability which has at its core impact on students' standards of attainment. Wider aspects of achievement are also important – inclusion, aspirations, motivation, self-confidence – but all impact on attainment. It is, in general, higher attainment that secures better life chances for youngsters.

Local authorities are already judged on their capacity to make an impact on pupil outcomes. They have begun to develop and implement strategic planning in response to the publication in 2004 of the government's flagship policy *Every Child Matters*. The key elements within this policy are:

- Generating greater cohesion to provision for children and families.
- Bringing together children's services and education.
- Helping children and young people to stay safe and healthy.
- Supporting young people to achieve more highly.
- Enabling all young people to contribute to society and achieve economic well-being.

The implementation of these plans will be a real challenge for those involved to balance their revised extended remit with the drive for ongoing school improvement.

A significant statement by the government to reflect its overall educational direction came in its publication of the *Five Year Strategy for Children and Learners* in July 2004. Within this there were clear signals relating to the personalizing of leaning through the provision of increased flexibility and choice. On secondary education it stated that

> *Our central purpose for every pupil over the next five years is to raise the quality of education, teaching and learning, and to widen the range of real choices which are available. We will build on the achievements of the last seven years, to increase freedoms and independence; to accelerate the pace of reform in teaching and learning; and to extend choice and flexibility in the curriculum. Underpinning each of these is sustained and rising investment in schools.*

And, when providing more detail about education for students aged 14+, the paper calls for

- *A much wider choice of what and where to study, with high standards in every subject and new sixth forms and sixth form colleges where they are needed*
- *Demanding courses for the most able pupils, whether they take academic or vocational options, and Young Apprenticeships that start at 14*
- *Closer link between schools and employers, so vocational learning means something in the world of work*
- *Extra support for young people leaving care*
- *High-quality advice and guidance to help young people make good decisions, and a wide range of things to do and places to go for young people outside school or college.*

Of course the paper also contained details of the drive for more specialist schools and academies together with the Building Schools for the Future programme and the development of a New Relationship with Schools to reduce the burden of bureaucracy. Nevertheless, a clear statement was being made about the need for less central control and direction of the curriculum and teaching and learning, and the development of a system more capable of responding to diverse needs.

At the time of writing the government's current White Paper, *Higher Standards, Better Schools for All*, is the subject of much controversy around the issues of Trust Schools and admission arrangements. Nevertheless, the paper recognizes that personalization is at the heart of solving the key learning challenges facing the education system, and in particular those relating to the poor performance of students from low socio-economic groups and ethnic minority communities.

Arguably the accountability framework for the government and its agencies is most keenly experienced every five years via a general election. But that is too blunt an instrument for measuring success or failure and it does little to add value to schools and others who are attempting systematic reform to scale, in other words demonstrating significant impact on those currently experiencing failure. Rather the DfES too needs to consider the consequences of its policy-making in relation to measuring its impact, particularly on those students currently not well served by the system. School improvement is most often measured in the DfES at whole-school level, meaning that we work within a system which is differentiated between schools that may be successful, coasting, underperforming or failing. Such an approach can obscure the considerable variation in student outcomes that exists within the majority of schools. Personalization must be accompanied by frameworks of accountability that reflect a more sophisticated view of impact. This must ensure that the work of all players is focused in the right area and that it is playing its part in delivering an effective personalization agenda.

We have already said that teachers have always used a variety of strategies to try to meet the needs of different groups of learners whether these be the highest or lowest attainers, boys or girls or different ethnic groups. Nevertheless, it is fair to say that those in practitioner roles have not always felt that their efforts have been consistently supported at all levels of the system. There has been something of a disconnection between those working with children in classrooms and those removed from that direct interaction. Often government ministers and officials refer to the 'front line' when talking about teachers and other classroom-focused professionals. The term itself captures something of the flavour of the relationship between those groups and the perceived hierarchy in policy-making. Those with the least direct contact with students and schools take the biggest decisions about how resources should be deployed.

Increasingly the 'front line' is being asked to make decisions locally about how best to bring about solutions to learning challenges. And yet there is no new infrastructure in place to support a dialogue or interface between policy-makers and practitioners. Teachers can best judge for themselves the extent to which they feel represented in discussion or consultation about policy developments, and the extent to which they feel their professional associations perform this role for them.

More recently the government, through the development of the national strategies, focused on the challenge of raising attainment through the development of approaches and resources to support the enhancement of classroom practice. This has met with some success and has helped to bridge the perceived gap between policy-makers and practitioners. By and large teachers have welcomed the development of a sound range of classroom-related resources through the Key Stage 3 Strategy; and the teams of National Strategy consultants, experts in the fields of maths, science and English teaching and learning strategies, working within local authorities, are seen in the main to provide good quality classroom-based support.

The challenge now is for each component of the system to work together with a high degree of coherence, transparency and professional trust to co-construct models of educational delivery which will personalize the experience each learner receives and so achieve a step change in the achievements and attitudes of young people.

The purpose of this book is to explore what the particular contribution of each component within the system should be to the personalization agenda. In addition how can these components support the ongoing generation and dissemination of more new knowledge which will in turn fuel the improvement of the education system.

Chapter 2

The need for change: from incrementalism to transformation

Levels of attainment

In the first term of the Labour government national standards for education were established against which student progress at ages 7, 11 and 14 could be measured. Since that time there have been some dramatic improvements in the number of pupils achieving the expected standard in national tests at all levels in the education system. Major financial and human investment has been made in the national strategies for literacy and numeracy and the government has claimed that there is hard evidence of improved outcomes to demonstrate that progress has been made.

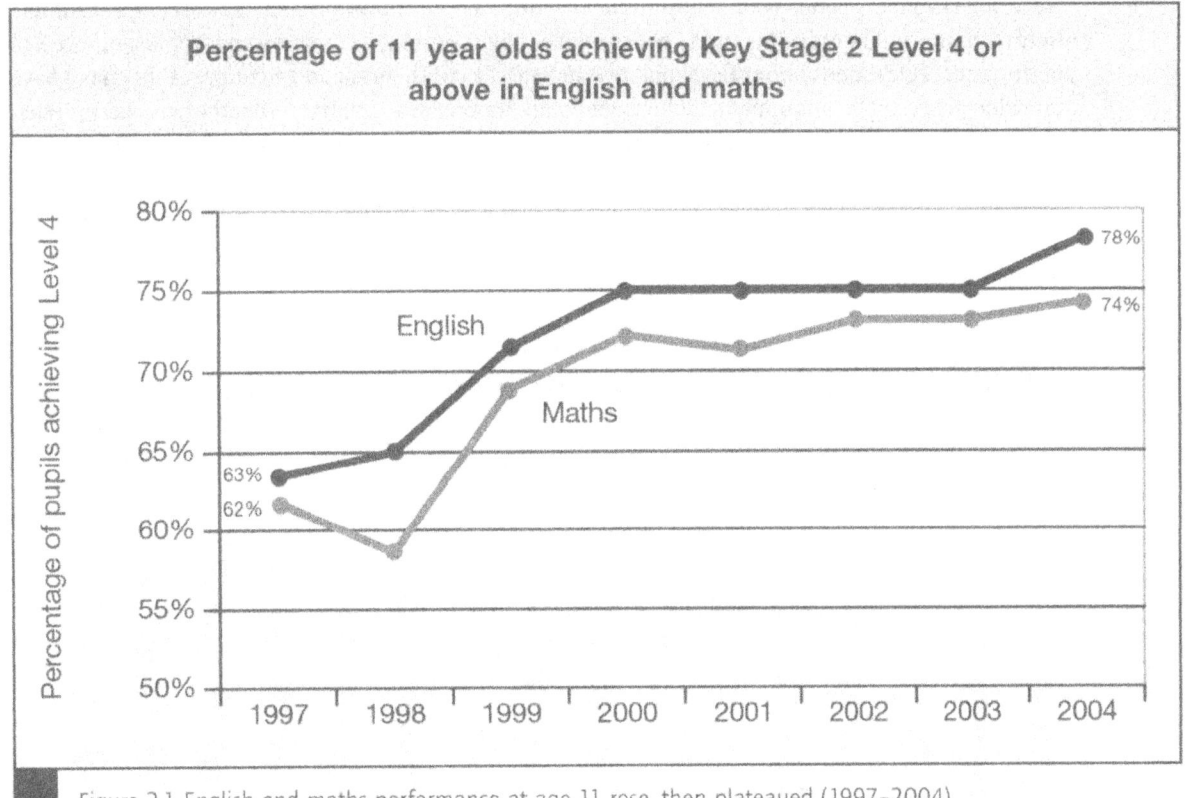

Figure 2.1 English and maths performance at age 11 rose, then plateaued (1997-2004)

Figure 2.1 indicates a dramatic rise in standards by the end of Key Stage 2 between the years 1997 and 2000 although more recently improvements have plateaued somewhat. Figure 2.2 illustrates a similar pattern at the end of Key Stage 3.

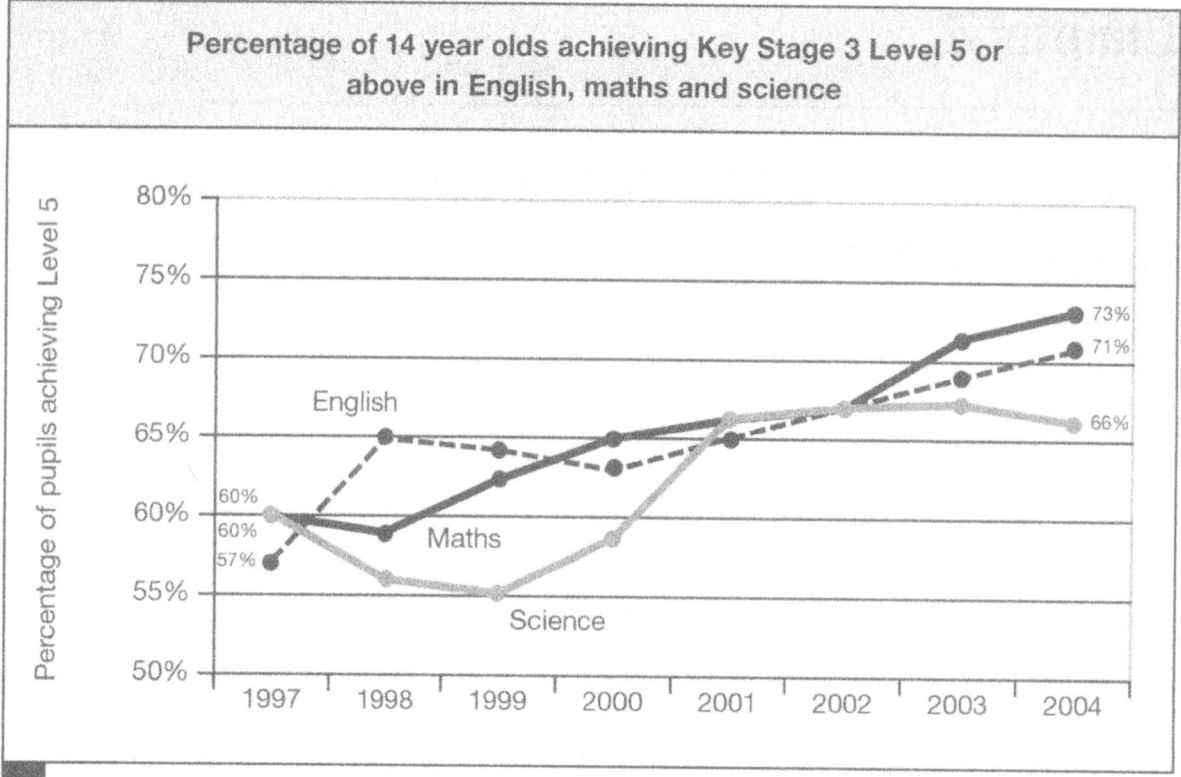

Figure 2.2 Improvements in English, maths and science, at age 14 (1997-2004)

Nevertheless many people both within and beyond the education system question the headline interpretation of the results and believe that they provide a misleading representation of performance. Questions about the reliability and validity of the tests and the impact they may have on wider aspects of attainment, achievement and motivation persist. Whether we accept that argument or not it is irrefutable that even within the current official figures there remain some major challenges to the issue of how to generate a transformational improvement in standards. When looking at Key Stage 4 the data (Figure 2.3) indicates that the percentage of pupils gaining five or more higher grade passes has increased over recent years but that increase has been incremental at best and the step change hoped for and expected has not materialized.

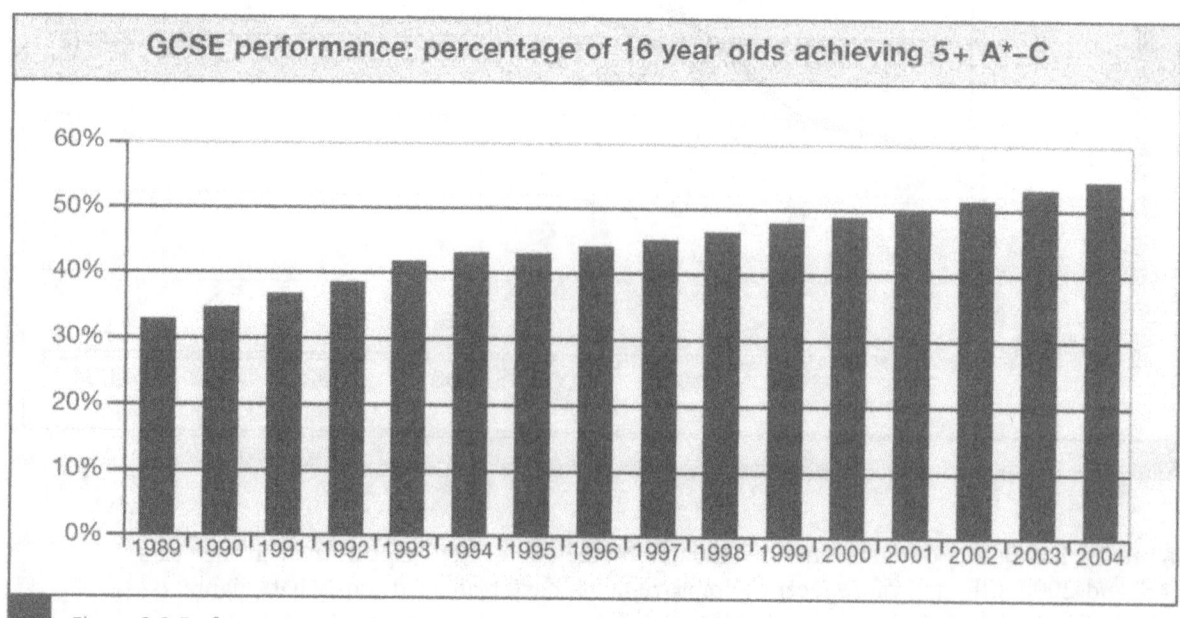

Figure 2.3 Performance at 16 has increased incrementally

Around 25 per cent of 11 year olds are still not gaining the expected standard in basic skills and 38 per cent of 16 year olds fail to achieve five higher grade passes at GCSE; 5.4 per cent of students leave school with no qualifications at all. In addition, figures estimate that over seven million adults currently lack basic literacy and numeracy skills.

Moreover, Figure 2.4 illustrates the variation in attainment at GCSE higher grade pass level related to parental occupation. The clear message is that some groups benefit significantly more than others from what is currently offered by the mainstream school system.

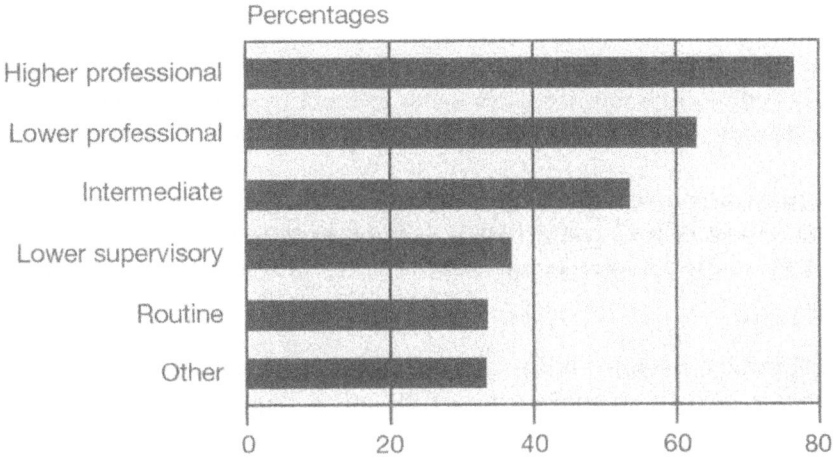

Figure 2.4 Percentages of pupils from different parental occupation groups attaining five high grade passes

Equally, we should be in no doubt about the consequences for later life of doing well or less well within the education system. As Figure 2.5 indicates, high attainment has a direct impact on the likelihood of being in employment and securing high earnings.

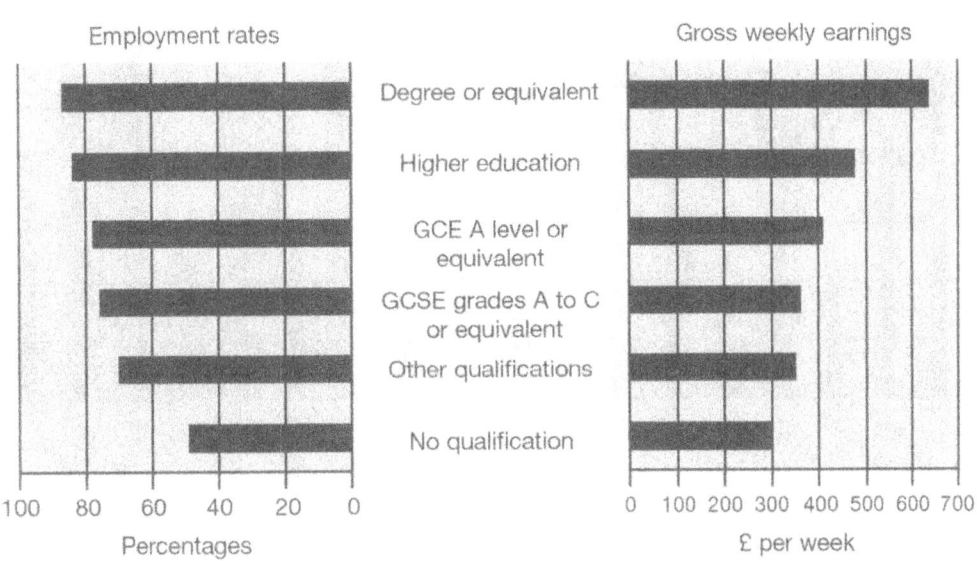

Figure 2.5 Impact of education level on earning capacity

The social class attainment gap

No one can doubt the importance of generating social cohesion within our society. The human, social and economic costs of creating groups of citizens who remain on the margins of mainstream society are there for all to see. Currently there are too many significant minorities who are excluded from enjoying the benefits of succeeding within the education system and so have little or no investment in the core structures, systems and values which are at the heart of everyday life. Any glance through data relating to student performance reveals the nature of the issue. In 2005 the DfES published its Community Cohesion Standards and, not surprisingly, within this it stated that the closure of the attainment and achievement gaps were at the heart of the issue.

Research from the OECD demonstrates that of the most productive nations economically England can of course claim some successes. Many of our 15 year olds perform well in terms of literacy, science and maths when compared with those in 25 other OECD nations.

However, England falls down when comparing the trailing edge of attainment with other countries and our social class attainment gap is one of the most severe – twenty-first out of 26 nations. Moreover, the gap is long-standing and successive government policies have struggled to influence it.

Poor white and black Caribbean children are often the lowest performers at GCSE. Figure 2.6 illustrates the variation in attainment across the different groups in our society with an emphasis on the impact of poverty and ethnicity. It is a picture of a system failing to meet adequately the needs of many children.

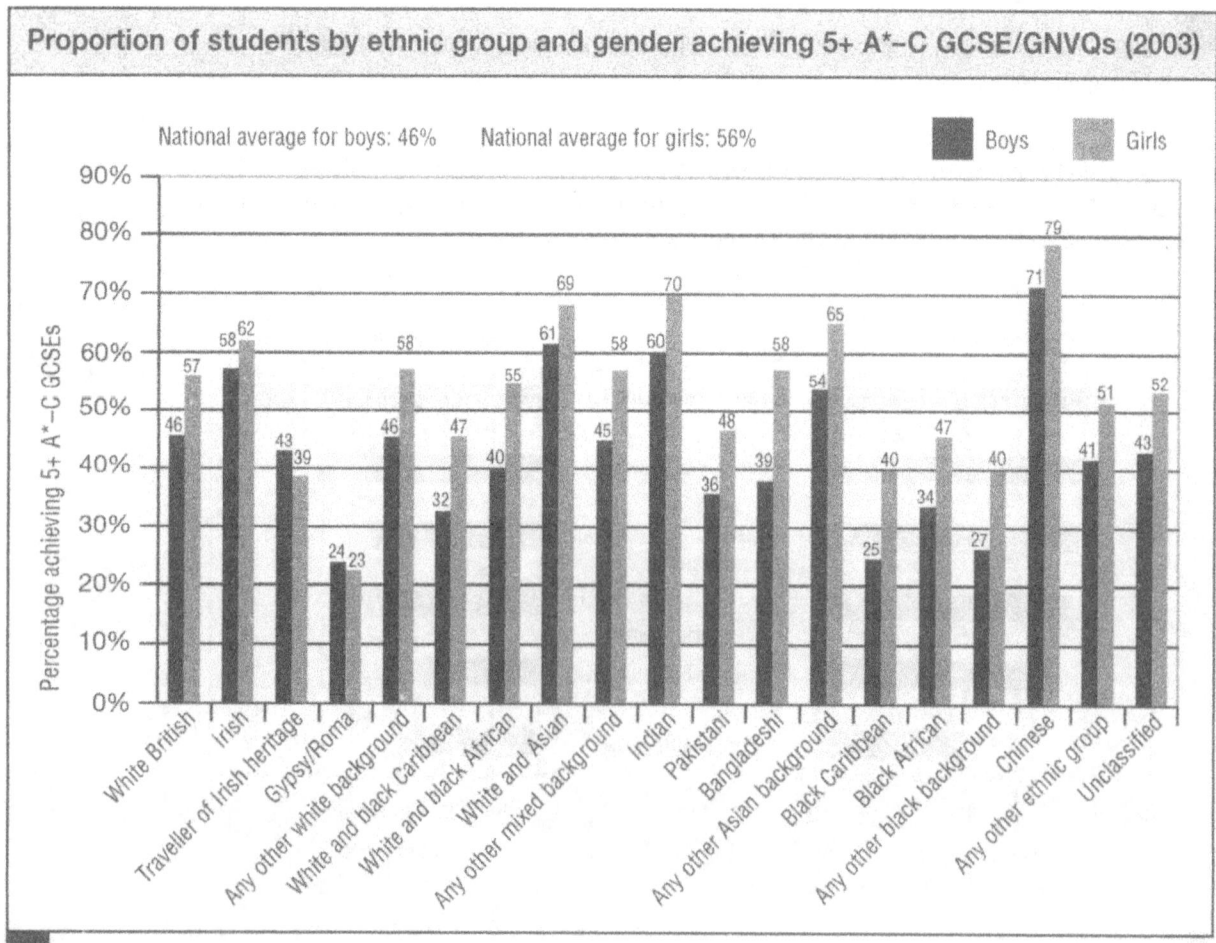

Figure 2.6 The attainment of students by ethnic group

Interestingly of course there are schools which are able to buck the trend. One such school is Preston Manor in Brent, London (see Case Study below). The school achieves very high standards in students' performance with an ethnically diverse pupil profile.

The school is very focused on teaching and learning and in particular in supporting student self-esteem through encouraging student participation and actively promoting student voice. It provides an excellent example of how, by understanding the nature and needs of the learners and using this to tailor the offer, high levels of engagement and performance can be achieved.

Another school that has achieved success in a similar context is Valentines High School in Redbridge in Greater London (see Case Study on page 16).

These two examples indicate that where schools find ways of responding better to the needs of learners what can seem like intractable problems can be solved.

Case Study

From October 2003 to September 2004, a team of students from Preston Manor, Alperton, Copland and Queens Park schools in Brent worked with Blaze Radio and the National Youth Theatre to produce *The Manor*, an innovative radio issue-based soap opera and website designed as a learning resource for the PHSE and Citizenship curriculum.

The work was designed as part of the collaboration activities that the schools undertake in partnership with one another, and was decided on through consultation with the students.

It was felt that the issues that arose naturally when devising drama with students in this way could form the basis for an excellent resource for teaching PHSE and Citizenship, and that a soap opera and website developed towards this aim could then be disseminated to a wider audience across the web. After securing funding for start-up from the DfES Innovation Unit, *The Manor* began in October 2003.

In the execution of their project students designed and constructed a website using cutting edge technology to promote interactive aspects of the site.
They presented live performances, including a performance at the Lyric Hammersmith in London and took their work to a number of local schools in a series of roadshows.

Staff identified a number of learning outcomes which they have monitored regularly throughout the project.

Learning outcomes

Students creating the soap opera developed their:

- Speaking and listening skills.
- Use of improvisation for the development of plot and character.
- Understanding of plot and character development.
- Reading skills.

- Writing of dialogue in script format.
- Understanding of media industry and production roles.
- Ability to work independently and in groups.
- Live performance skills.

Technically, the students also developed their:
- Understanding of radio drama technique.
- Use of microphone.
- Understanding of sound effects and music to create atmosphere.

Students building up the website developed their:
- Speaking and listening skills.
- Ability to work in groups and define their own roles in relation to one another within those groups.
- Research skills.
- Understanding of interactive multimedia production and consumption.
- Understanding of web authoring, design content and usability.
- Understanding of Flash animation and Adobe.

Case Study

The aim of the intervention at Valentines High School in Redbridge, Greater London involves peer mentoring between Year 11 and Year 9 students of African and Caribbean origin – because this group does not achieve as well as other groups. It has been a conscious decision to employ a black training and consultancy company to help set up the programme and conduct the training of the mentors during phase one of the intervention. It is hoped that this will provide a powerful symbol for the students as they work with successful black male role models.

The programme has been devised to focus on such issues as academic work, raising self-esteem, promoting positive attitudes to learning, increasing aspirations, developing independent learning skills, increasing awareness of issues related to black underachievement, positive behaviour management, time management, organizational skills and encouraging the group to support each other in the process of setting and achieving targets.

In order to track progress teacher and pupil questionnaires were devised based on a point system. English, maths and science teachers, tutors and heads of year were required to complete these questionnaires. The data would be used to feed into the mentoring sessions and would help provide the basis for the targets set. The pupil questionnaire requires the pupils to self-assess and then compare their perceptions against their teachers' perceptions. This has led to the Year 11 students increasing their understanding of the teachers' role (leading to more mature responses in their learning) and it has also encouraged the Year 9 students to reflect more openly about barriers and successes in their learning.

Outcomes of the work

- Reduced incidents of poor behaviour in target group reported by subject teachers, tutors and heads of year.
- Increased motivation reported by subject staff and students.
- Year 9 value positive black role models in Year 11 and external provider.
- Students welcome the fact that the school has faced this issue rather than shy away from it.
- Students feel the school has recognized their need for a positive identity within the student body.
- Open and positive dialogue between black students and project staff regarding how the school can support black students in the future – with the help of black students.
- Improved levels/grades – although the mentoring phase needs to operate for longer than a term to reap the benefits identified by research into educational gains to be achieved through mentoring programmes.
- Greater awareness among students of issues facing black students and how they can work positively with staff and with each other to overcome potential barriers.
- External provider's report cites 'outstanding level of commitment' from Year 11 mentors with increased skills in communication, target-setting and problem solving. A test set by the tutor on mentoring procedures and skills 'displayed a level of knowledge on paper that demonstrates a high level competence in their understanding of the concepts and theories of mentoring (peer mentoring)'.
- Students say that 'the interaction between year groups brings the school closer together' (Year 11 student).

Figure 2.7 also illustrates the impact of socio-economic well-being on student performance. The fewer students entitled to free school meals in a school the more likely it is that a greater number will achieve five or more higher grade passes. This is another clear indication of the system not meeting the needs of significant numbers of learners.

Quite clearly, in general the poorer you are the less your chances of success within the system and if you're black the same difficulties apply. The personalization agenda must have the addressing of this issue at its core.

Attitudes to learning

In addition to measures of low attainment, indicators of ambivalent attitudes to and lack of engagement with learning on the part of significant numbers of young people of all abilities suggests that many fail to maximize their true potential. This, if nothing else, represents a loss of human capital to the nation.

Increasingly across the system, schools are incorporating students' views and their preferred learning styles into the way they are developing the curriculum in order to promote personalization.

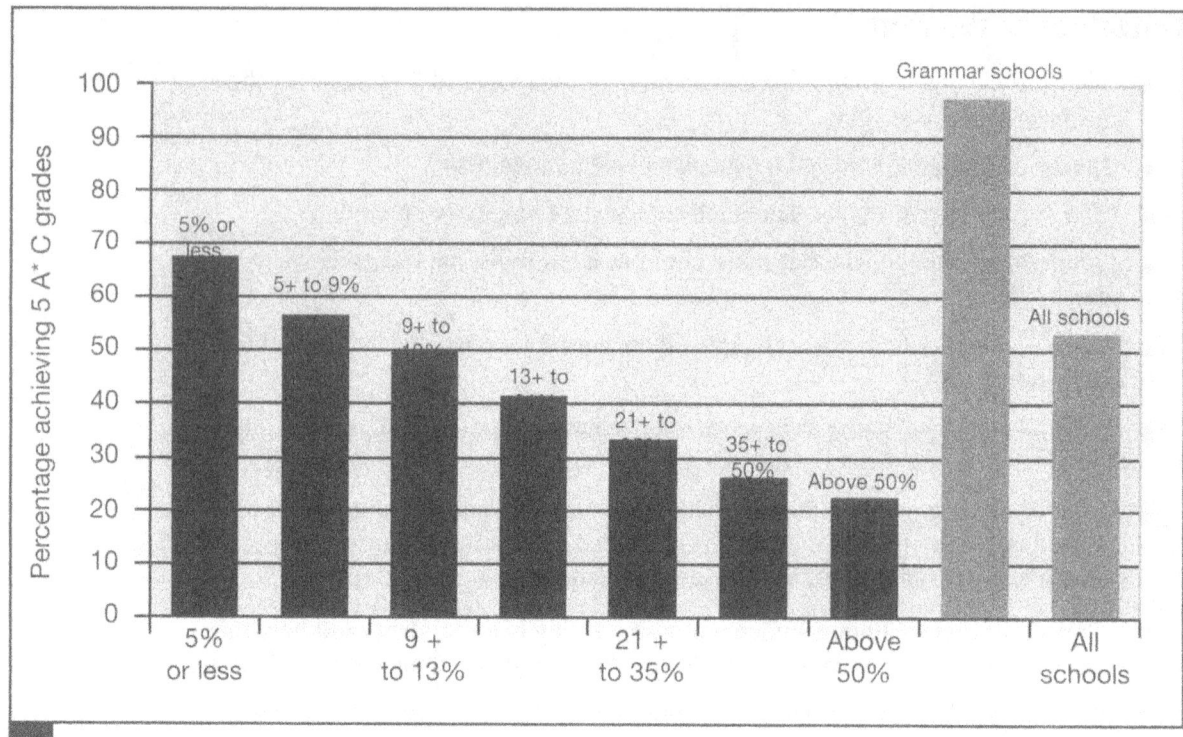

Figure 2.7 Percentage of pupils achieving 5+ A*-Cs at GCSE according to FSM band, 2002

Significant benefits of this approach have been reported. Schools are using the development of student voice by engaging students both within individual schools and across partnerships in a variety of ways. Examples include:

- Some schools are attempting to measure student perceptions and attitudes before, during and after the work.
- Holding joint training sessions between staff and students where they work together on learning styles and culture.
- Extending student involvement by visits to other school – the cultural barriers and differences can prove challenging. One partnership of schools has found it more successful as a first step to switch the staff between schools, to get an understanding of the different expectations and attitudes of the students.
- Using student voice as the route to addressing problems: for example an online survey of bullying has yielded useful information.
- Students observing lessons and providing feedback on teacher performance can be a useful input into staff performance management and departmental reviews, and the student response to this involvement is very positive.
- Exit surveys from leaving students – these can be a source of useful feedback.

The National Foundation for Educational Research (NFER) and other organizations can provide a range of tools to support the incorporation of student voice into planning and organizing the education offer. Examples of instruments include those relating to

- perceptions of the purpose of school
- the value of school
- qualities of good teaching

- what motivates students to learn
- attitudes to homework.

The following series of statements (National Collaborative 2006) is taken from a group of schools trying to generate increased motivation for students in science in Key Stage 3 and could be used in any subject. Students are asked to tick one of a series of given responses to indicate their views. The statements are:

1. I enjoy most lessons in this subject
2. My teachers think I am good at this subject
3. My teachers make this subject interesting
4. I can achieve my target in this subject
5. Lessons in this subject are easy to understand
6. This is the hardest subject I have to study
7. This subject will never be useful to me when I go to work
8. When I leave school I can see me using my learning in this subject
9. When I leave school I can see me learning more about this subject
10. I like finding out how this subject is used in everyday situations and in industry
11. Girls find this subject easy
12. Boys find this subject easy
13. It is more important that boys do well in this subject than girls
14. Girls find this subject more difficult than boys
15. Doing things practically in groups is the best way to learn topics in this subject
16. Pictures and diagrams help me learn easier than words and sentences
17. To help me remember facts it is better to always copy them out
18. It is easiest to learn in this subject by doing reading about the topics that my teachers tell me to read
19. Learning is easiest when I work on my own
20. Videos and computer simulations are much better than hearing explanations about the topic from teachers

At Park House School & Sports College in Berkshire they have developed a strong emphasis on seeking the views of their students to inform key curriculum and teaching and learning decisions. They use questionnaires to illuminate issues relating to:

- attitudes to learning
- attitudes to teaching
- self-esteem
- life in school
- preferred learning styles.

This information is then analysed systematically and used alongside performance data to produce a more personalized experience for all students.

Local authorities are also making use of attitudinal surveys. One example, in Hull (Hull Lifelong Learning Partnership 2005), revealed that of the 16–19 year olds surveyed

- 25 per cent of pupils sampled left school with no qualifications
- only 38 per cent felt school was interesting
- 22 per cent thought their secondary education had been poor
- 43 per cent felt it would be difficult to find a job in the local area.

Current data relating to truancy confirms that many young people feel that the education system as it stands has little to offer them.

Recent statistics confirm that despite a range of government measures the average number of pupils missing school each day increased by 5,000 during 2005. These are the highest figures since 1994. Unauthorized absences have grown to 1.25 per cent, an increase of 0.12 per cent.

The conclusion must be that there are too many losers within the system as it currently functions. A major challenge is to close the gap in pupils' achievement and raise levels of motivation by improving the offer to all. In doing so the education system can be a powerful force for connecting all groups with the benefits society has to offer.

The needs of business and industry

Over recent years the business community has made it clear that in their view there are significant shortcomings within the current education system. Failure to produce correct skill sets and attitudes, it is claimed, is damaging the ability of the commercial sector to be both sufficiently productive and competitive in the twenty-first century.

Recent pronouncements from the Confederation of British Industry (CBI) confirm this. Their employment trends survey in 2005 confirmed that 42 per cent of employers were unhappy with the basic skill levels of school leavers and 50 per cent believe that there are significant shortcomings in the areas of communication, team working and problem solving. The then Director General, Sir Digby Jones, also commented that with only just over half of all 16 year olds achieving a C grade in English and maths, and a reduction in pupils succeeding in modern foreign languages, 'the system is failing teenagers, taxpayers and employers'.

In the same local authority quoted above a similar picture emerged with employers noting the following shortcomings in the skills of applicants for jobs which were leading to significant recruitment problems:

- practical skills – 63 per cent
- technical skills – 45 per cent
- communication skills – 36 per cent
- numeracy skills – 35 per cent
- literacy skills – 37 per cent
- problem solving – 33 per cent
- computer literacy – 24 per cent.

How can personalization address the needs of both the learner and their prospective employers in a coherent way? In this book, we suggest some possible routes to answering this question.

Subject-specific issues

It can be argued that the economic well-being of the nation depends to some degree on the ability of the education system to ensure that a sufficient quantity of very able young people are sufficiently interested in particular subjects to motivate them to pursue them at university and into careers. The Higher Education Funding Council for England (HEFCE) has described what it terms as a number of Strategic and Vulnerable Subjects. These include mathematics, a range of science-related subjects and aspects of technology. HEFCE argues that a lack of interest in these areas is storing up a crisis for the nation.

The Roberts Review of 2002, *SET for Success – the supply of people with science, technology, engineering and mathematics skills*, has identified an undersupply of scientists in the future in the UK. There is already an endemic shortage of specialist science teachers. The rapid pace of scientific and technological change requires a scientifically literate public and yet interest in the field of science remains at a low level. This lack of interest in these areas may well be developed through students not relating positively to the subjects as they are experienced through secondary education. For example:

- attainment levels in science at Key Stage 3 are lower than maths and English
- they are lower than those attained at the end of Key Stage 2
- fewer pupils attain a C grade or better at GCSE in science than in maths or English
- the take-up of science at A level was lower for all sciences in 2004 than it was in 1998, the decrease over the period being as follows:
  - biology 7.1 per cent
  - chemistry 11.8 per cent
  - physics 14.5 per cent.

In 1994 4,100 people applied to study chemistry at university, but by 2004 the figure had dropped to 2,400.

There is a clear need to provide pupils with a more motivating and relevant experience of science within the curriculum.

When taken together the above issues lead us to the conclusion that the need for change is irrefutable. There is without doubt a reservoir of talent and energy within our schools and society that is not being realized by the education system. The question is how can the drive for personalization be a key part of the solution to the problems the education system currently exhibits.

Chapter 3

Policy and action

The customization of public services

After more than two terms of the Labour government there can be no doubt that there has been considerable investment in education to fuel the knowledge economy. But ambivalent attitudes to learning and to making a personal investment in education remain among too many of the population.

Back in 2002 the Labour government set out its principles for reform in all sectors of public service – high standards, devolution, flexibility and choice. These principles have been developed by the government into an approach to public service delivery across all sectors. It is important to see the personalization agenda within the context of this wider policy framework as it is reflective of what is widely described as a commitment to a needs-led model for all public services. Briefly stated these principles are:

- *Universal provision with personalized delivery*

  Universal on the basis of need and not on the ability to pay, and personalized by being shaped to individual need. There has been a pledge to move away from the post-war welfare state where 'one size fits all' and to move to a service designed to meet the needs of individual pupils, parents and citizens. This means that the government's aim is to create a system in which services are geared to the lives of citizens rather than being governed by the decisions, customs and behaviours of service providers.

- *High standards flexibly delivered*

  The government would like to be able to demonstrate that standards of public services have risen and that setting national standards has been key to driving improvement. But they recognize that this drive has to be combined with the flexibility to cater to particular local and individual circumstances. They see that such an approach requires a new relationship between the centre of government, where policy has been traditionally created, and local organizations. They have a stated intention to draw on expertise locally to contribute to policy development, target-setting and 'communicating with citizens'.

- *Equity and choice*

    The government has asserted that extending choice will improve service quality and deliver greater equity. The assertion is based upon a recognition that exercising choice will require greater responsibility on the part of the individual. In future, individuals will need a real say over the services they want and how and from whom they are delivered. This is reflected in the White Paper published in October 2005 (see page 27) in which the emphasis on parental choice is a central theme.

In its election manifesto of 2005 the Labour Party further developed these themes into a set of aspirations to tailor education to the needs of the individual learner. The policy drive for personalization recognizes that many schools have striven to tailor their curriculum and teaching methods to meet the needs of students. But too often the best of this practice is locked up in a single school, or subject department or even in a single classroom. So how can the government support the growth of a high quality universal system of education that is able and equipped to meet the complex needs of twenty-first-century learners?

The trend towards flexibility and diversity in education

The *Five Year Strategy for Children and Learners*, published by the Department for Education and Skills in 2004, sets out certain principles for reform. In his foreword to the document the then Secretary of State, Charles Clarke, asserts that greater personalization and choice will be at the heart of better public services and higher standards. The strategy confirms that up to now choice has been available only to those who could afford it – the challenge is to provide choice and quality for everyone. The fact is that some education consumers are better able – either through economic or intellectual power – to exercise choice.

The government also recognizes the risks involved in providing parents and pupils with greater choice. For public services choice represents a challenging concept if it is coupled with equity. Some in education have argued that choice will only become a reality once there are sufficient surplus places available in schools to enable parents and children to choose between them. In policy terms this represents an impossible demand and therefore choice has to be encouraged and interpreted in a different way.

Choice has to be made more widely available to students and parents through combining and recombining existing school organizations together with partnerships beyond the school, and harnessing the capacity of all stakeholders to add value to what's on offer. For example, when pupils transfer at transition from primary to secondary many of them suffer set-backs. In future those groups of pupils and parents most vulnerable to such set-backs need to be offered timely and appropriate support. New forms of information are being made available to parents and pupils – in particular value added data that can support better understanding about net gainers and losers in any single school.

The *Five Year Strategy* and the *Every Child Matters* agenda both set high aspirations for pupil outcomes in the future.

The overarching aim of the five year strategy is that there should be in every part of the education service and in every phase of learning:

- A stronger voice for children, young people and adults in the development of policy and the design of services.
- Services and learning designed around the needs of the individual and available at a time and place and in a form which suits their needs.

- Better advice and information to enable people to make choices.
- Better support and incentives, particularly where financial barriers would work as a disincentive to participation.
- High minimum standards for everyone, irrespective of who they are or where they live.

But the drive for these aspirations also recognizes the limitations of centrally prescribing processes or of relying on bureaucratic and burdensome forms of accountability. Such policy levers belong to the last decade described elsewhere as informed prescription.

As part of the developing policy context, the DfES along with Ofsted is creating a lighter touch infrastructure to support a new relationship with schools. Part of the intention is to cut back on bureaucratic burdens. This is exemplified by a commitment to:

- Fewer interventions from the centre; more focus on outcomes and less prescription of detailed processes.
- Fewer separate funding requirements and funding streams where possible; more scope for local people to set targets which match local need and to use resources flexibly.
- Streamlined systems of audit and inspection.
- Information collected once and then made available in a form which can be used many times by different players in the system.

Moreover, there is no one model for realizing the government's ambitions. In the past universal provision has failed to meet the needs of individuals where it has sought to impose a single solution.

The current response to these policy aspirations is to set a shared vision for personalized education provision in the future and an infrastructure that enables schools to work together and to work with other stakeholders to make the goals of high excellence and high equity a reality for all.

So the most practical way for the system to promote choice in compulsory education, where providers are largely predetermined, is to offer a series of different routes through the system.

Permitting curriculum diversity

The tight grip of the government on the curriculum, which has characterized the education landscape for much of the last two decades, is being relaxed in recognition of the fact that greater diversity of provision is needed if standards are to increase. The picture of a rather limited one-size-fits-all model has been modified to stimulate and encourage a broader offer to students. The key building blocks in this quest for diversity are:

- The opportunity to condense Key Stage 3 into two years or less.
- The creation of a 14–19 curriculum with differentiated pathways.
- An increased profile and status for the vocational curriculum.
- The creation of a range of specialist schools within a local area.
- Encouraging effective partnerships between schools, colleges and business.
- Support for schools to work collaboratively to share expertise and to create greater diversity.

Informed professionalism

During recent years the government's education policy has increasingly recognized the importance of informed professionalism as a fundamental driver in the quest for school improvement. During his time at the Department for Education and Skills as Head of the Standards and Effectiveness Unit, Michael Barber created a framework for analysing trends in educational reform since the 1970s and this illuminates how each successive decade has been characterized by a very different view of the nature of the teaching profession. It describes a profession moving from being 'knowledge poor' to 'knowledge rich'. Within this movement each decade exhibits different features.

The 1970s are seen as a time when many teachers were enthusiastic and committed to the care and welfare of their pupils but ultimately this boiled down to committing a series of random acts of kindness with little impact on standards. To many this may seem a gross misrepresentation of a time of significant curriculum development (remember resource-based learning where for the first time many teachers devoted much energy to increasing the range, quality and diversity of educational resources available to pupils in classrooms!). But it was a time when teachers had little access to data to inform classroom practice and the standards agenda was largely invisible.

Barber views the 1980s as a period of uninformed prescription, when the government lost faith with the profession and took it upon itself to impose a series of reforms which were not based upon any evidence about what was likely to have a positive impact on standards and quality. The most far-reaching of these was the development and implementation of the National Curriculum.

The arrival of the Labour administration in 1997 saw the introduction of the literacy and numeracy strategies, both of which were based on tried and tested developments in other parts of the world. This was the period of informed prescription where teachers were trained to deliver the strategies to support them in being more effective in the classroom. There began a debate about whether changes in classroom practice would benefit learners.

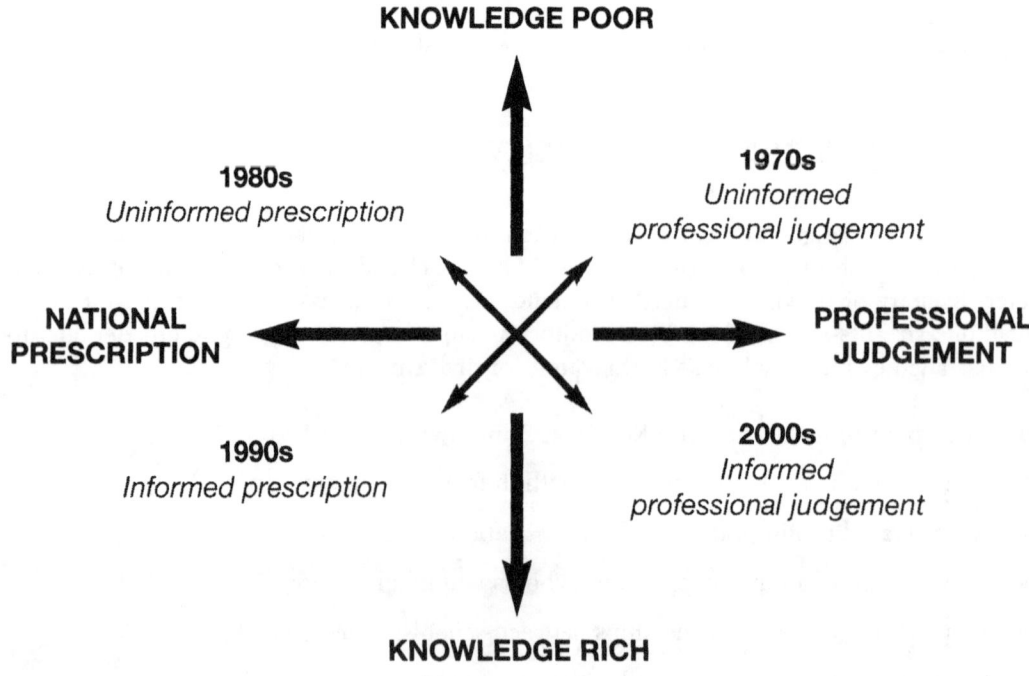

Figure 3.1 The journey to informed professionalism

The beginning of the current decade saw the dawn of what Barber terms as informed professionalism. Teachers' professional judgement was to be the basis of the next phase of reform. As a policy position, informed professionalism is predicated on a number of key assumptions or beliefs:

- Expertise to raise standards lies within the profession.
- Practitioners are motivated by a strong moral purpose.
- Sharing effective practice provides for professional renewal.

The next stage of secondary reform

The government White Paper released in October 2005, *Higher Standards, Better Schools for All*, makes clear the government's commitment to personalization:

> *Personalization is the key to tackling the persistent achievement gaps between different social and ethnic groups.*

The Paper contains a range of strategies for injecting funding into the system to support a greater tailoring of provision to meet the needs of diverse groups. These include:

- increased resources to support raising the attainment of ethnic minority students;
- expanding gifted and talented provision;
- improved literacy and numeracy provision;
- expanding provision beyond the school day;
- increasing the number of specialist SEN (special education needs) schools.

The Paper also envisages all schools to be part of partnerships aimed at improving the quality of provision. The Education Minister Jacqui Smith has said (DfES, 2005b):

> *The next stage of secondary reform will see schools increasingly working with other schools and institutions; where individual schools contribute, through partnerships and other networks, to best meet the personalized learning needs of all pupils in a community.*

Schools which are designated as High Performing Specialist Schools will be expected to exemplify the following characteristics and ways of working:

- Placing partnership at the heart of all they do.
- Become drivers for local collaboration.
- Capitalize on their own strengths.
- Draw on the strengths of other schools and institutions.
- Innovate and design solutions to challenges.
- Raise attainment within and beyond their own school.

The policy context in which all schools are now operating is one in which all systems and structures are there to serve the learner by better meeting their needs and so raising standards. The challenge to schools – and to the system – is how to develop effective methods of collaboration to achieve the goal. In truth this is not as simple as it may sound. Collaboration is both resource and trust hungry. There will be a pressing need to discover and replicate how this is best achieved.

Chapter 4

School partnerships driving personalization

In any system attempting to bring about personalized learning for each and every learner there needs to be a recognition and understanding of the part played by schools working in collaboration. Despite the apparent tension in the system of league tables, and the consequent competition this is seen to engender between schools, for many years there have been ongoing discussions between headteachers and senior leaders in schools often with local authority co-ordination and leadership. Many schools see advantages in being part of a loose network of professionals and in the secondary sector heads and school leaders have worked alongside each other sharing common issues and seeking common solutions. Schools are in the forefront of recognizing that in trying to offer an increasingly personalized experience for learners or a more tailored curriculum, they are more likely to maximize their chances of success if they collaborate with others. But this approach is insufficiently rigorous if the desired outcome is a system which narrows the achievement gap and raises the bar for all learners.

Why current government policy is encouraging partnership and collaboration

A number of current initiatives have been established to encourage schools to work collaboratively in pursuit of higher attainment for pupils. These include Leadership Incentive Grant Collaboratives, aimed at strengthening leadership to improve teaching and learning; Performance Collaboratives, which link high performing schools with schools where standards are low to exchange practice; and Network Learning Communities whose purpose is to build a knowledge base about successful school networks. These initiatives are predicated on the belief that the national literacy and numeracy strategies have been highly successful in raising standards for students but for a number of reasons (not least the findings of recent research) it is widely accepted that the impact of the national strategies has plateaued.

The response of policy-makers has been to create funding streams that seek to support schools working together to collectively address some of the seemingly intractable systemic issues of underperforming students. Nationally the trailing edge of underachievement shows that the same groups of students are performing below their peers year on year.

There is significant evidence that for many students the curriculum offered in schools and the testing regime that stems from it creates positive experiences for large numbers of learners to make progress. However the sophistication of data now available clearly demonstrates that for some students the experience on offer in our schools is not conducive to achievement for all. Equally it is clear that some schools develop particular successes with particular groups of students, or in particular subjects or across a particular Key Stage.

The challenge is to create ways of sharing that success more rapidly. And to do so in ways that inspire teachers to seek ongoing improvements in their own practice. School improvement and school effectiveness research has consistently demonstrated that teachers who continue to improve their practice do so best when they work in schools that encourage staff development through sharing aspects of teaching and learning.

Many of the solutions to meeting the needs of the majority of learners in our schools lie in the hands of the successful classroom practitioners within our schools and with those who are willing to take calculated risks with their practice to develop, try out and evaluate innovative ways of working. The only effective way in which this existing and developing expertise can be transferred and replicated throughout the system, so that all schools can develop effective personalization, is for the education system to create a successful and sustainable infrastructure for collaboration.

From competition to collaboration

Until recently heads and school leaders have frequently argued that the driving forces in the system have encouraged competition between schools rather than collaboration. In particular they cite the pressures of league tables as a reason for competing. But for many teachers sharing practice is part and parcel of their professional values.

Many teachers say that they gain from learning alongside other teachers despite the pressures of league tables. They are keen to exchange methods of teaching and learning across common subject areas and with a focus on the particular challenges that they face in their classrooms.

At the same time, there is a growing understanding and knowledge about the diversity of learning needs and learning styles of individual students and groups of students. If schools simply continue to offer the same diet to all their students then it is unlikely that they will manage to meet the needs of those learners. And few schools possess the range of expertise they know they require in order to do so. Even where schools are outstanding high performers in overall school performance, they are becoming increasingly responsive to the benefits of working in partnership with other schools near to them and serving the same geographic communities.

Sharing expertise within and between schools

Schools are responding to these challenges in a number of ways. In some schools teachers are organizing teachers' learning groups to exchange practices across staff and to generate new teaching and learning strategies. In other schools new roles have been developed such as learning development officer whose key function it is to organize and operationalize the systematic sharing of effective practice. For many the key to sharing practice lies in using data to illuminate where in the curriculum there seems to be effective practice. Schools are becoming increasingly skilled at using the available data to identify variations in performance across different subjects by the same students or groups of students. It is incumbent upon leaders and managers in schools to pursue these within-school variations to discover what is happening – or not happening – in those classrooms where students are attaining higher standards or making the greatest progress. This is, of course, one of the keys to effective personalization – finding what provision best meets the needs of particular kinds of learners. A reasonable course of action might be

> *Judging by the performance of x students in y activity you are teaching those students really well. Could you lead a whole staff session to explain what you feel the key factors contributing to success might be.*

As schools increasingly establish structures that support the benefits of sharing practice among their own staff they are beginning to value the opportunities offered by partnership working. Many schools are scaling up their approach to whole-staff development to incorporate the exchange of practice across institutions. In some circumstances a high performing school will work to support another which is clearly struggling. In other circumstances there is little difference in overall school performance but different pockets of expertise in each school.

Teachers will identify that in a collaborative environment between schools each school may have a slightly different issue with a slightly different cohort, but by agreeing to focus on a shared challenge they are able to share practices that all teachers will then use as classroom interventions, tracking students' progress and sharing evaluation of impact. In other words learning what works most effectively with particular groups of learners.

Some examples of shared learning challenges include:

- *Raising the attainment of boys*

    In Cambridgeshire the Bassingbourn Village College Partnership of three schools has been working on a joint project to improve the engagement and attainment of boys. A steering group has been established, a plan prepared and the work is moving forward with high status across the three schools.

- *Improving motivation in science at Key Stage 3*

    The Haybridge High School Partnership of three schools in the Midlands is creating a database of good practice in science teaching and learning through a programme of peer observation. A DVD has been produced to support CPD as well as the creation of a coaching programme.

- *Increasing aspirations in modern foreign languages*

    In Nottingham the Fernwood Partnership of six schools has developed a range of strategies for increasing the engagement of students at both Key Stage 3 and 4. Several cross-school teacher-led projects have produced measurably increased confidence and a rise in attainment.

- *Developing a coherent 14–19 programme*

    The Penair School Partnership of four schools in Cornwall has developed joint working on 14–19 provision where new vocational courses have been constructed, improved relationships established with post-16 providers and a greater range of extra-curricular provision created.

- *Improving the engagement and attainment of ethnic minority students*

    In Redbridge the 11 schools which make up the Valentines Partnership have been working collaboratively to develop strategies to raise the achievement of groups in a multi-ethnic context. A community forum has been established and a Community Languages conference held. Community mentors work with students across the partnership and a range of effective teaching and learning strategies are being shared.

What systems and structures facilitate effective collaboration?

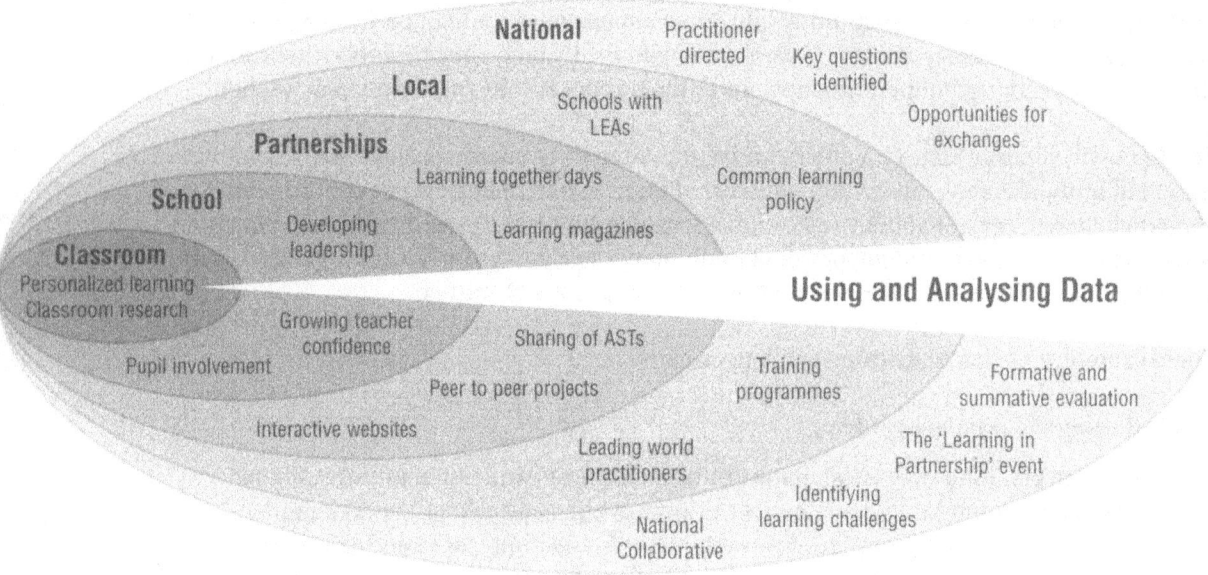

Figure 4.1 A system model to support personalization through collaboration

The model in Figure 4.1 describes the components and processes which can work together to achieve more effective personalization. To establish cross-partnership working, structures need to be put in place to secure that effective opportunities happen. Many groups of schools have established a role of partnership co-ordinator to implement the work and ensure that it is followed through consistently and rigorously.

But a constant question is how best to quality assure what practice ought to be shared? There is still a tendency among schools to share practices which may seem to be interesting or even innovative without sufficient emphasis on or evidence of a positive impact on learners.

Nonetheless, there is a great deal of progress being made in evaluating the effectiveness of specific interventions. Understanding the connection between teaching and gains in attainment is paramount if teachers are being expected to share and replicate their teaching and learning expertise. And they need the right climate, infrastructures and enabling school leadership if they are to do this. Increasingly teachers are examining the impact of their practice – its efficacy with particular students – and how it makes a difference to their motivation, engagement and progress. In some partnerships schools have created 'activist' posts open to a member of staff who wants to pick up an issue to do with teaching and learning and run with it both within and beyond their own school. Other partnerships have created joint appointments such as an advanced skills teacher (AST) post or someone to manage pupil data across a partnership.

Most importantly though teachers consistently say that they have to have dedicated time to make exchanging practice realistic. This needs to be planned ahead – often by a year or more so that staff resource is allocated to ensure that key staff have timetabled contact time with one another. Shared timetabling might also enable a particular group of students to be brought together for team teaching or enable the deployment of specialist subject or vocational teaching across the partnership. In many partnerships students are being timetabled for lessons in partner schools or colleges to better meet their particular interests or learning need. From the experience of schools working together in this way a series of particular practices can be identified and offered as a model for working.

A model for building effective collaborative practice and personalized learning

A number of common elements and characteristics are emerging from those schools working collaboratively in pursuit of higher attainment for learners and the personalization of the curriculum. There are two main premises which inform this way of working:

- that students' standards will be raised through partnership working with a focus on personalization;
- that practitioner expertise about tailoring teaching and learning will be enhanced through partnership working.

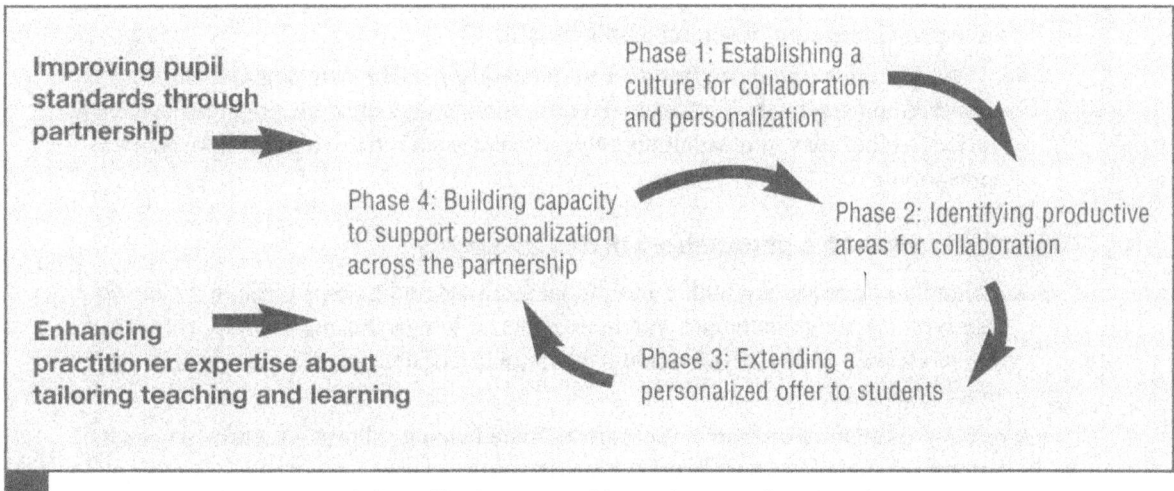

Figure 4.2 Four phases to building effective partnerships and personalized learning

The key features of the model shown in Figure 4.2, which describes how a group of schools might approach building a partnership, are:

Phase 1: Establishing a culture for collaboration and personalization

- The senior leadership team in each partner school needs to model the values and ethos that they wish to engender across participating schools. A culture of openness and professional trust has to be developed from the outset at all levels in the partnership to ensure sustainable working relationships. It's important that teachers and others including support staff invest in the endeavour and develop a shared sense of ownership.

- A culture and climate for improvement needs to be based on explicit and shared professional expectations and reciprocal accountability – born out of mutual professional respect and equity.

- The focus for the partnership needs to be clarified – and the nature of the learning challenge to be addressed. The partnership activities that will best support greater personalization need to be identified in relation to the needs of particular individual learners and to groups of learners.

- Sharing data across schools about student performance, different curriculum models, staffing structures, staff deployment and resource allocations are essential steps in building insight into what's working most effectively and what's not. And interrogating the differences is part of growing professional knowledge about better meeting the needs of students.

Phase 2: Identifying productive areas for collaboration

- Develop understanding between practitioners in each school and across schools about the effectiveness of particular strategies of teaching and learning in relation to individual student outcomes and in particular to their attainment. Analyse the patterns of performance – use value added data to interrogate the links between socio-economic indicators, gender, students from ethnic minority groups, feeder primary schools and prior attainment.
- Identify which schools in which subjects seem to be doing well and which schools in which subjects are adding less value to student outcomes.
- Agree specific areas for collaboration where practice to support personalized learning can be shared on the basis of what's worked for the benefit of students and staff. Many schools have learned that for some staff a programme that personalizes their professional development needs is the best approach to meeting the personalization of teaching and learning.
- Involve students in developing an understanding of their own learning and the way it's being assessed. Students need to know about their own preferred learning styles so that they can develop strategies that work for them and offer support to one another.

Phase 3: Extending a personalized offer to students

- Identify and prioritize which individual students and groups of students face the greatest learning challenges by identifying the low performers. It's important that this is within a shared vision about the context of demographic factors such as employment routes.
- Analyse the nature of their underperformance using qualitative measures such as attitudinal surveys as well as quantitative data.
- Create a single team of key practitioners across the partnership with clear roles and responsibilities for tailoring teaching and learning. Postholders in middle leadership have a key role to play alongside others, including support staff.
- Agree timetable opportunities for classroom coaching/shared teaching/ collaborative planning and so on.
- Regularly track the impact of classroom interventions on identified student groups.
- Monitor and evaluate processes and outcomes with students and practitioners.

Phase 4: Building capacity to support personalization across the partnership

- Create manageable and sustainable opportunities for exchange between staff.
- Identify and share the cultural and technical change elements that have been effective. Many partnerships have developed extranets or web links between the schools within the partnerships, to pool resources and ideas to support personalization.
- Share exploration of raised levels of pupil engagement.
- Systematize the learning principles across the partnership ensuring sustainability in individual schools and across the partnership.

Developing self-evaluation for partnership working

Through working in this way schools are now beginning to address shared approaches to partnership self-evaluation. A systematic and rigorous approach to this is vital if important knowledge about successful practice is to be captured and transferred so that more students benefit from personalization. Recent developments in The Leading Edge Partnership

Programme, where several hundred schools voluntarily completed a common framework for reporting on their progress, demonstrates that there is an appetite in the profession for learning from what works with particular kinds of learners.

This approach to evaluation had four key purposes:

1. To support partnerships of schools working in this way, because there is little experience in this area.
2. To promote a consistency of approach to maximize the value of the findings.
3. To gather evidence about what schools choose to collaborate on.
4. To gather evidence of the impact of partnership working on the experience of students.

The self-evaluation framework encouraged partnerships of schools to pool their shared reflections of success in relation to

- their agreed strategic objectives designed to raise students' standards;
- the progress they have made in one year towards realizing these objectives;
- the challenges of working collaboratively;
- the solutions that are emerging to these challenges.

Initial findings from this project suggest that when schools have the opportunity to work together they choose to put their collaborative energy into learning together about successful and innovative classroom practice. Out of the 103 partnerships of schools involved, 97 devoted their energy and resources to the following areas:

- sharing pedagogy
- sharing schemes of work
- sharing subject training
- team teaching
- team planning
- classroom observation.

In addition, 92 per cent of those involved judged themselves to be making good or excellent progress with their objectives.

Collaboration is not straightforward. It is resource-hungry and requires high levels of organization. Schools identify four main barriers to sharing practice through working together but also highlight the levers that can make it work.

Barrier One – Difficulties in generating time

Levers for success:

- Video conferencing, email.
- Plan meetings well in advance – place on school calendars at the beginning of the year.
- Ensure that non-contact hours overlap to support working together, for example a working group team have one day's cover per half term; they agree a common meeting/working time across the partnership.
- Create a consistent pattern of the school day across the partnership.
- Hold joint INSET days.

Barrier Two – A lack of capacity

Levers for success:

- Strong senior leadership.
- Appointing people explicitly to commit their energies to collaborative projects.
- Create protected non-contact time for key staff.
- Appoint additional staff so that identified key staff can be timetabled less, with blocks of time available to provide support without cover implications.
- Create a partnership co-ordinator role in school to work in all schools in the partnership.
- Appointment of resource assistants to deal with administration.
- Appoint staff who are shared between the schools, including non-teaching staff, to work across the partnership.
- Use of advanced skills teachers across the partnership.

Barrier Three – Difficulties in managing conflicting priorities

Levers for success:

- Ensuring that the partnership work has a unique but vital focus.
- Focus on initiatives where the need for improvement is shared.
- Develop projects that are sustainable without the need for large amounts of additional finance.
- Focus on short-term projects.
- Use School Improvement Partners to jointly identify key areas of concern.
- Limit the number of core activities for partnership work.

Barrier Four – Problems in sharing effective practitioner experience

Levers for success:

- Creation of a partnership website to facilitate communication and information exchange.
- Creation of a Virtual Learning Community (with material that can be adapted so that it works in different contexts).
- Produce a directory of best practice in hard copy for distribution.
- Target dissemination at various levels within schools.
- Create a team of staff who work at different levels in respective schools, including middle leaders.
- Create subject networks.
- Joint timetable planning.
- Training offered across the partnership.

Only by supporting practitioners to share what best meets the needs of different learners in differing contexts can true personalization be achieved. Enabling the creation and development of effective partnerships, networks and collaborations is fundamental to realizing a personalized system of education.

Chapter 5

The power of data

A new role for data

The government, schools and local authorities are data-rich. Over recent years there has been a significant growth in confidence and competence in the ways in which we can harness data to the school improvement agenda. From the early days of target-setting for schools, the use of centrally generated PANDA information, the increase of value added data and the development of local authority data systems, we now have access to a vast array of information about performance.

Until relatively recently the prime function of the use of data has been to make judgements about the performance of local authorities, schools, subjects and of individual teachers. This is fine as far as it goes but it does little or nothing to contribute to the personalization agenda.

All suppliers and users of data must move to a position where the prime function of data is to enable us to understand better the needs of learners, how effective the provision we make is for them and how that provision can be enhanced. For data to feed the transformation and personalization agenda effectively it should be used to provide the system with information about what works in what context with what kind of learners.

We are now fortunate enough to be working in a context where the data available to us is increasingly sophisticated and is therefore capable of telling us a great deal about how effective we are being with individuals and with groups of learners with particular characteristics. If the key purpose of using data can now be seen to be to support our efforts to enhance the experience and provision for learners, it is important to establish what are the key elements of data available which need to be used by different groups within the education system and how this can be used to support the drive towards a more personalized provision.

Contextualized data and personalization

The increasing availability and use of performance data, which takes account of the context of students' background and circumstances together with their prior attainment, provides a perfect vehicle for us to illuminate how different components of the school experience impact upon the performance of different types of students. We can now develop a relatively secure evidence base which relates to:

- prior attainment
- ethnic grouping
- socio-economic circumstances
- gender.

On the basis of all these factors we can generate reasonably reliable estimates of student performance moving into the future. The challenge is now not simply to use these tools to make judgements about performance but to feed our understanding about how to change what is offered to best fit the needs of learners.

Asking the right questions

It seems to us that by asking a different set of questions it is possible to use the data in such a way that it will help the system share and develop the successful practice which already exists within it, in order that what works for particular types of learner can be replicated and scaled up for the benefit of all. These questions include:

- Where within a school is there significant variation in performance between learners with similar characteristics?
- Are there instances of these differences within the same subjects and/or between different subjects?
- What are the differences in content and process in the situations which might be making significant contributions to the differences in performance?
- Once illuminated, can the differences which appear to be generating success be transferred and replicated elsewhere?
- What are the implications for resourcing and for professional development of this replication?
- Are there aspects of content/process which might need to be eliminated?
- How can this be achieved?

It is the case that the first two questions are often asked as a matter of course. The subsequent ones are less commonly addressed. The example used here is that of a school. But of course in the pursuit of system-wide personalization it can be argued that these are the questions which need to be posed both within local authorities and nationally.

The case for an action research model

The Leading Edge Partnership Programme, which is funded by the Innovation Unit at the DfES, has pushed further the notion of a more rigorous approach to exploring, identifying and sharing what strategies are effective with particular groups of learners. A key part of its work is to support schools in developing innovative approaches to raising the attainment of those students who are underperforming in the lowest 20 per cent of attainers.

In order to generate an evidence base which can provide some secure information about whether or not the approaches being trialled by schools have any positive impact on the target groups, the Programme has worked with the Fischer Family Trust (FFT) to produce a suitable data model. The aim is to illuminate which ways of working appear to have the greatest positive effect on particular groups of learners.

In this project the schools' innovations have been categorized into a series of interventions as follows:

- using assessment to raise attainment
- improving behaviour
- sharing curriculum practice between schools

- sharing staff training
- using pupil voice
- student mentoring
- staff coaching
- using data to impact on classroom practice
- developing active learning.

The Fischer Family Trust worked with the project to produce a data set which enabled the schools to identify the students who would be the beneficiaries of the interventions and to note on a spreadsheet similar to Figure 5.1 the particular type of intervention they were using with the students.

	A	B	C	D	E	F	G	H	I	J	K
1	FFT_ID	UPN	SURNAME	SURNAME_ALT	CFIRST	COTHER	DOB	GENDER	CURR_SCH_ID	INTERVENTION	
2		X12345678900	Mango		Michaela		18/05/1991	F	9994004		
3		X12345678901	Grapefruit		Ashley		24/01/1991	M	9994004		
4		X12345678902	Peach		Daniel		11/03/1991	M	9994004		
5		X12345678903	Strawberry		Thomas		09/05/1991	M	9994004		
6		X12345678904	Mango		Adam		15/04/1991	M	9994004		
7		X12345678905	Orange		Maria		23/09/1991	F	9994004		
8		X12345678906	Apricot		Megan		10/08/1991	F	9994004		
9		X12345678907	Crab Apple		Elizabeth		21/05/1991	F	9994004		
10		X12345678908	Banana		Leon		04/01/1991	M	9994004		
11		X12345678909	Thyme		Timothy		04/02/1991	M	9994004		

Figure 5.1 Spreadsheet to identify intervention students

The FFT material also enabled schools to benchmark the students in terms of what the expected attainment of the children would be notwithstanding any impact from the project work. These expectations were based on a range of contextual data and provided estimates for all three core subjects (Figure 5.2).

	A	B	C	D	E	L	M	N	O	P	Q	R	S	T	U
1	FFT_D	UPN	SURNAME	SURNAME_ALT	CFIRST	EN5_EST	EN6_EST	ENG_EST_SCH	MAG_EST	MA5_EST	MA6_EST	MAG_EST_SCH	SCG_EST	SC5_EST	SC6_EST
2	10004	X12345678903	Strawberry		Thomas	99%	74%	36.5	40.1	100%	93%	37.3	38.4	99%	83%
3	10007	X12345678906	Apricot		Megan	98%	65%	35.6	38.2	99%	82%	35.5	35.7	95%	58%
4	10010	X12345678909	Thyme		Timothy	96%	55%	34.6	38.1	99%	81%	35.4	36.7	98%	69%
5	10009	X12345678908	Banana		Leon	94%	44%	32.9	36.2	96%	62%	34.2	34.1	89%	38%
6	10003	X12345678902	Peach		Daniel	93%	42%	32.8	34.1	87%	36%	32.1	32.2	75%	18%
7	10008	X12345678907	Crab Apple		Elizabeth	81%	20%	30.2	31.9	69%	15%	29.8	30.7	58%	9%
8	10006	X12345678905	Orange		Maria	74%	14%	29.2	34.4	89%	40%	32.4	32.4	77%	20%
9	10002	X12345678901	Grapefruit		Ashley	62%	8%	26.8	30.8	57%	9%	29.3	27.8	26%	2%
10	10001	X12345678900	Mango		Michaela	37%	2%	24.3	29.3	41%	4%	27.8	26.1	14%	0%
11	10005	X12345678904	Mango		Adam	22%	1%	22.6	26.7	18%	1%	25.2	26.8	18%	1%

Figure 5.2 Pupil estimates in the core subjects of English, maths and science for the end of Key Stage 3

The hope was that the work might illuminate which kinds of activity seemed to be having most impact on, say, white working-class boys, middle-class girls from lower attainment bands, black African Caribbean boys and so on. Such illuminations would then assist practitioners to personalize and tailor provision to their needs.

The work is at an early stage of development and is of its nature experimental. Nevertheless, 8,500 students were involved in the first phase of this work and their performance was tracked via the 2005 Key Stage 3 tests to ascertain whether their involvement in the interventions might have made a difference to their performance and, more importantly, whether particular types of intervention appeared to be more powerful in raising attainment.

Conclusions drawn from the analysis of the available data are tentative and yet that analysis does reveal some tantalizing signposts in terms of value added performance. For example:

- Value added for students with interventions was generally higher than for those not involved in interventions.
- The differences between students with interventions and other students are more noticeable for Level 5+ than for Level 6+. This is not surprising given that the aim of the programme was to focus upon students with relatively low prior attainment.

Table 5.1 indicates the differences in value added (VA) in the core subjects for boys and girls of similar prior attainment involved and not involved in interventions. The shaded boxes indicate where the differences are significant.

Indicator	Boys					Girls				
	Non Intervention		Intervention			Non Intervention		Intervention		
	Pupils	VA	Pupils	VA	Diff	Pupils	VA	Pupils	VA	Diff
English L4+	527	+6%	623	+10%	+4%	264	+5%	269	+12%	+7%
Reading L4+	743	-5%	905	+3%	+8%	407	-7%	423	+2%	+9%
Writing L4+	413	-3%	464	+1%	+4%	186	-9%	176	-1%	+8%
Mathematics L4+	408	-2%	411	+7%	+9%	334	-2%	331	+4%	+6%
Science L4+	477	+1%	482	+10%	+9%	401	+1%	370	+8%	+7%
English L5+	1052	+1%	1283	+5%	+4%	633	+1%	692	+2%	+1%
Reading L5+	1428	+1%	1722	+4%	+3%	984	+1%	1129	+4%	+3%
Writing L5+	1267	+3%	1509	+6%	+3%	863	+4%	978	+3%	-1%
Mathematics L5+	772	-3%	912	+7%	+10%	780	+2%	825	+6%	+4%
Science L5+	968	+1%	1165	+4%	+3%	996	+1%	1092	+3%	+2%

Table 5.1 The impact of interventions on attainment

In terms of trying to ascertain which particular interventions were more powerful than others the data suggests that the greatest gains were made where schools focused their energy and resources on:

- Sharing curriculum practice, resources and staff training between schools.
- Using data to impact on classroom practice.

This is, of course, work on a relatively small scale but it seems to us to point the way to a more sophisticated strategy for using data which can inform the personalization agenda. It can help us to know what we should be providing for particular learners because the evidence shows it works, and equally what we should stop doing because the evidence shows it doesn't. It supports schools in making decisions about how to make the most effective use of scarce resources. Findings from this kind of research, if shared and replicated, could be part of the answer to tailoring provision more closely to the needs of learners. This is what we might begin to refer to as development of the science of personalization.

There are many inspiring examples of individual schools using data in innovative ways to discover the effectiveness of different ways of working on particular learners.

At The Thomas Hardye School in Dorchester groups of low-attaining students were exposed to a range of new strategies relating to assessment for learning, the setting of homework and experimental classroom seating arrangements. Students were benchmarked before the implementation of the new strategy and every four weeks during the programme. Graphs were produced and the relative impact of each strategy assessed.

We have already highlighted some of the work being developed at Park House School & Sports College in Berkshire (see page 19). Here a partnership database has been established which can be accessed by all teachers, enabling them to identify where practice is successful with different types of learners. Once successful practice has been identified it is then shared across the schools so that all students benefit.

At St Thomas More Roman Catholic High School and Norham Community Technology College on Tyneside a 'traffic light' system which indicates the degree of progress students are making in relation to available performance data has been introduced. Again this enables teachers from both schools to identify effective practice and to replicate it in other contexts.

The key point here is that we are witnessing a major shift in the way in which data can be used. Increasingly its focus is and should be to support the personalization of the curriculum offer and teaching and learning strategies.

What should the government be doing?

The strategic role of government in this is potentially very powerful. As part of its programme of working with data it needs to devise strategies which build on the above work to generate significant intelligence about those ways of working which appear to meet best the needs of different groups in our schools. Once that knowledge has been captured there should be a targeting of resources to enable the replication and scaling up of successful practice across all schools. This shift in the role of data from being fundamentally judgemental to being instrumental in a professional identification of what works will be a significant step forward towards personalization.

Chapter 6

Harnessing the strength of business and industry

The old model

Good schools have always tried to make effective links with local businesses and industry. A variety of activities ranging from work experience to industry days and enterprise activities have to a greater or lesser extent enhanced the experience of young people and generated an understanding of the world of work. In some cases businesses have given elements of their staff time to take part in activities to enhance literacy and numeracy provision or by providing mentors for both students and staff.

Although of course there are exceptions, by and large such activities were in effect bolted on to the regular curriculum. Many were at best ad hoc and in the worst cases had little or no relation to the day-to-day educational provision. They were an added extra rather than an integral part of what the system had to offer learners.

The need for a new relationship with new responsibilities

Our theme in this book is that it is only when all key stakeholders in the system come together in a coherent way to play their part in delivering a personalized experience, and rise to their responsibility to deliver professional expectations, that the education system will be transformed. Business and industry are key stakeholders. A previous chapter demonstrates the stake they have in the system. The challenge to this group is how they can work strategically with education practitioners to make best use of the resources they have available and help create an improved curriculum experience for all learners. It is in the interest of society as a whole that each component of the system recognizes that it has its own unique responsibility to develop the potential of our young people. Indeed, it may be by focusing their resources on the needs of particular groups that business and industry will have most impact. A former Education Minister commented:

> *Employers constantly tell me that some school leavers still lack basic competence in areas like literacy and numeracy, and many more lack the other so-called 'soft' skills of problem solving and the ability to work with others. I believe that we need to re-orientate what is on offer in schools to ensure young people are enabled to acquire these skills, which are important for life as well as for work, and for society as well as the economy. In addition, we have to secure a wider choice of different courses and different learning styles from which they can find what best meets their needs.*

Capacity issues in schools

The expanding range of career opportunities and the increasing reliance on advanced technology within many employment areas means that it is impossible for schools to have the capacity within their own resources to understand and communicate to students the nature of the world of work and how the make-up of the curriculum relates to it. Indeed, the danger is that the rapid pace of technological advancement in many businesses and industries could be perceived by some students as rendering much of what takes place within the curriculum as being increasingly irrelevant to many learners as they view their career aspirations.

This explosion of technology in the world of work is potentially a powerful resource in the journey to discover how to enhance the capacity of the education system to enrich the curriculum offer to students and so increasingly personalize provision. The motivating potential in particular of digital technology, digital media and a range of industry-standard expertise and equipment can play a major role in transforming the system.

A new model for business and industry partnership

The challenge presented here is for representatives of business and industry to work together with education practitioners to co-construct learning experiences which motivate, engage and better meet the needs of learners. These experiences need to be integral to the curriculum and be seen to feed in to improving motivation and raising levels of attainment. They may also be expected to raise the career aspirations of particular groups of learners and connect them more strongly with learning in particular and with society generally.

Some examples of innovative practice

The following three examples give some idea of the many different ways of incorporating innovative practice in schools.

1. Dream Ireland

In Northern Ireland a company called Dream Ireland has been working with schools and the education authorities to generate projects which bring together industry-standard digital media technology to energize the learning process for students. Their first venture into this work was DreamLab Generation which developed and tested ways in which young people (15–18) can further their skills in art, design, music and technology through programmes of production-based training, led by industry professionals, but taking place in school. It also explored how students, teachers and organizations can best cope with the rate of change engendered by digital technology.

Recognizing that traditional approaches to learning in the classroom are not necessarily the best way to prepare young people for careers, nor to provide young people with the range of skills and aptitudes required by industry in the knowledge-based economy, DreamLab Generation has developed new learning models that put the young person first and broaden their horizons, aspirations and abilities, while helping teachers and schools adapt to the impact of digital technologies upon the way we learn, work and are entertained.

> *There is a new generation of young people who are already interacting with technology, creating digital art, websites, 3D models, animations and playing games on consoles, PCs and mobiles in their bedrooms, before they even enter a classroom ... these are the next generation of entrepreneurs and business people who, faced with outdated learning content in the classroom, are in danger of becoming disengaged*

> *from learning in traditional ways. DreamLab Generation is addressing this need. Digital technologies are inherently transferable in the knowledge-based economy, not only across the creative industries but also within more traditional sectors of the economy ... but it is also the attitude towards learning and the creative process which DreamLab Generation impacts upon for young people, helping them think in new, creative ways.* Gary McCausland, Director, Dream Ireland

The central innovation within DreamLab Generation was the manifestation of the concept that schools cannot function as 'sole traders', especially in relation to digital technology and associated skills. Previous approaches to this issue have been ad hoc and their outcomes perceived as hard to measure. This project approached the issues methodically while allowing the freedom and speed of movement that is necessary to retain the enthusiasm and attention of young people.

Although DreamLab Generation was primarily about models that are transferable and which offer equality of access across education environments it also recognized the need to point participants to career pathways – particularly in the case of exceptionally talented individuals. This project had the most profound impact on the young people involved and resulted in teachers developing new skills and working in innovative ways with business and industry.

Dream Ireland's latest venture, DreamLab Learning, takes the same concept and develops it further. It aims to create a formal, sustainable learning network for teachers and industry expertise within and across schools in Northern Ireland that is focused upon harnessing the power of industry standard digital media to reconnect with learning those children who could be described as 'hard to reach'. The network is focused upon defining, developing and refining a model which is effective and sustainable.

The project is deploying a range of approaches to learning that were developed during DreamLab Generation. These approaches are based upon integrating industry-specific skills, expertise and resources into the curricula framework. They make use of digital technologies in bringing technology, art, media, music and moving image together in the classroom. Its expected key outputs include:

- Increases in literacy and numeracy for students.
- Improved engagement and motivation with learning.
- Increases in digital skills for students and teachers.
- Creation of new and effective models of industry–education collaboration.
- New progressive pathways for both students and for teachers' professional and personal development.

2. Films for Learning (www.filmsforlearning.org)

At The Thomas Hardye School in Dorchester teachers have been working with professional film-makers to create resources for classroom use, to give teachers and students the skills to make their own films and to generate a better understanding of how to work with industry professionals. It provides an opportunity to see how working with creative consultants can enhance the curriculum experience.

There are few opportunities for teachers to produce first-hand authentic digital resources to fit in with their own classroom practice and that could be useful to their colleagues. This project encourages the production of new insightful first-hand teaching and learning resources with the added bonus of being communicated in a fast and empowering way.

The project is innovative not only in its use of new technology and approaches, but in its focus on empowering students as well as teachers to co-construct these innovative resources to serve the needs of learners. It is a powerful way of binding together the world of industry and education to make the curriculum offer more relevant and motivating for learners.

3. The National Collaborative

The National Collaborative project involves 20 secondary schools from across England in developing and sharing innovative approaches to the teaching of science and technology at Key Stage 3. The focus of the work is to raise standards for low attainers through enhancing the curriculum experience by including expertise from outside the world of education. The hypothesis being tested is that the motivation and performance of students will be increased by opportunities to personalize the curriculum offer through their exposure, as part of the regular curriculum, to 'real world' examples and applications of fields of study in science and technology. Examples of these collaborations between industry-standard organizations and schools include those shown in Table 6.1.

School project	Industry expertise
Crime scene investigation with Year 8 students	Neat 3D and Manchester Police
Advanced technologies, telemetry	The Defence Diversification Agency
Using SMART materials to motivate students	Qinetiq

Table 6.1 Collaboration between schools and industry-standard organizations

A key element of this project is to share across all the schools the successes and problems generated by working in this way so that any benefits can be replicated more widely. In order to facilitate this sharing, a web-based tool has been devised which enables teachers in each school to record the activities they undertake and the way they are tailoring their teaching and learning to better match the needs of specified groups of students. Through compiling a composite record of how a group of teachers in different parts of the country develop and implement their science and technology teaching, by working with industry professionals in different ways, the intention is to capture a model for replication and scaling up.

Examples of what the teachers within each school are addressing are as follows:

- Which aspects of the curriculum in science and technology will you develop in your school?
- What will be innovative about the content?
- What expertise do you need to broker in to enhance the innovative nature of the work?

- Which teachers do you need to engage with?
  - to capture learning
  - to replicate learning
- How do you transfer practice
  - from one teacher to another
  - one department to another
  - one subject to another
  - one school to another?
- What are the effective ways in which successful innovation in teaching and learning strategies can be replicated?
- What's the role of student voice?
  - How will you capture students' experience within your schools?
  - With students in other schools?

By recording their responses to these and other questions and sharing them on a dedicated website teachers are co-constructing at a national level ways of enhancing teaching and learning in science and technology. A particular challenge that needs to be resolved is how to make the content and pedagogy of both of these crucial subject areas more relevant and accessible to the real-life needs and interests of a diverse range of students. Only by looking beyond established school practice will it be possible to harness sufficient inspiration and technical knowledge to energize those learners who currently are not well-served.

Working with business and industry in this structured and strategic way will be a crucial part of developing the personalization agenda. Meeting the needs of all learners requires the system to significantly increase the range and diversity of what is on offer in a way which supports learners to be more motivated and so to achieve more. The role of business in this is fundamental. Schools do not have the capacity and cannot be expected to do this alone.

Chapter 7

Local authorities at the heart of personalization

Constructing a shared vision for personalization within the local authority

The specific needs of local communities will vary according to local context and shifting demographic and economic patterns. Local authorities need to establish a coherent and shared analysis of the challenges facing children and young people in their care. A significant part of this analysis will focus on the effective use of local and national performance data set alongside other indicators such as health, wealth and well-being.

A prime function of the local authority must be to bring together all key stakeholders in the local area to develop a shared vision for how the local system should be combining to better serve the needs of learners.

There are many examples of how they are doing this and indeed in many cases they are creating a vision for local services which extends into an extensive agenda embracing the need for local regeneration.

Developing an agreed strategy for meeting learner needs

The *Five Year Strategy for Children and Learners* sets out a role for local authorities as providing strong leadership for children's services and education. Local authorities will be at the hub of activity to support and protect children and young people with new Directors of Children's Services. And this direction is central to the development of a new partnership with local government. The agenda poses a challenging and complex brief and requires a clear strategic response to be articulated and implemented by local authorities.

The most successful and innovative authorities are already organizing their services to meet these challenges. Partnerships of schools will be a key component of service delivery and in many cases such partnerships are already at the heart of new forms of service delivery. Most importantly if such new forms of service delivery are to be successful in producing sustainable improvements in students' standards over time it is crucial that they are focused and rigorous from the outset.

Transforming services for personalization

In terms of the education sector some authorities have laid the foundations for transformation already. They have done this in a bid to create a culture of collaboration and partnership, engaging all stakeholders at every stage.

Key features of working in this way are to:
- Create opportunities to extend dialogue with headteachers and practitioners in schools and local authority staff at all levels.
- Seek ways of engaging parents, students and stakeholders in such dialogue.
- Focus on raising standards through teaching and learning as the key driver for system improvement locally and nationally.
- Identify strengths in schools and service delivery that currently meet different learner needs effectively.
- Identify and agree challenges and weaknesses locally in meeting the needs of all learners.
- Create and share a vision for students' entitlement to personalized learning in each community, in every school and in every classroom.
- Gather evidence of current practice that supports that vision and that delivers aspects of the entitlement.
- Devise a strategy for collaboration that makes a reality of sharing effective practice.
- Set shared targets, agreed outcomes, timescales and aspirations as part of the strategy.
- Allocate resources to best support priorities in raising standards.
- Monitor and evaluate progress with those involved, setting professional expectations and holding each other to account!

Where these approaches are being adopted new relationships are emerging between school leaders and local authorities. A key factor in sustaining and developing these relationships will be the capacity of all to continue to invest in shared decision making. Pooling school-level data is a powerful way of creating a sense of shared ownership in a collective endeavour.

In some authorities there has long been a moral commitment to ensuring the success of every school. This commitment now needs to be capable of being translated into action, whereby the services and resources available within the authority are put at the service of schools and other partners in such a way that they meet particular demonstrable needs.

The draft of *Spreading Information Across Local Authorities* (DfES et al., 2005) confirms that authorities face five key challenges in ensuring that local networks and partnerships maximize their potential in the drive to improve learning:
- Focus – making sure the strategic challenge is clear.
- Ownership – ensuring that all players understand and accept what is expected of them.
- Alignment – ensuring that funding streams are matched to priorities.

- Capacity – endeavouring to generate the resources necessary to meet the challenges.
- Effectiveness – developing the knowledge and understanding needed to get the best out of networks and partnerships.

We believe that the models developed in Chapter 4 of this book –

- a system model for supporting personalization through collaboration

and

- building and sharing effective collaborative practice

will be essential tools in creating a local authority in which personalization is successful.

Chapter 8

Key expectations for the system components

In order to ensure the delivery of personalization of learning we believe that the key players who make up the education system need to fulfil the following expectations.

The government should

- Continue to enable schools to explore flexible and creative solutions to local challenges by finding ways to relax curricular requirements wherever possible and appropriate.
- Use influence and financial support to encourage business and industry to invest in their future employees by working with education practitioners to create partnerships which enhance the education offer to learners.
- Continue to invest in successful partnerships of whatever nature which can demonstrate that they bring greater effective diversity to the curriculum on offer.
- Hold all parts of the DfES and all its agencies to account, that is, to ensure they focus all their resources and energies on supporting schools to better meet learner needs.
- Develop data strategies which are focused on identifying what works for learners of differing needs and developing ways of capturing, replicating and scaling up proven successful practice.
- Strengthen the capacity and requirement of local authorities to be key players in identifying successful practice and ensure that that practice is shared and adopted for the benefit of all learners in the locality, in addition to developing a shared vision for personalized learning across the authority.

Schools should

- Recognize that they are part of a broad system whose prime focus is to better meet the needs of learners in order to generate improved outcomes.
- Understand that collaboration with a range of partners is vital, if sufficient capacity for curriculum provision to meet the diverse needs of learners is to be generated.
- Develop a positive attitude to innovation in pursuit of solving learning challenges.

- Develop a sound understanding of the different learning styles of students and how that should impact on provision.
- Become expert at using data to better understand what practice is most effective with different types of learners.
- Create and support school leaders who develop a culture which puts student outcomes as the focus of all work and where an open-source culture thrives to enable the sharing of effective practice.
- Put student voice at the heart of school self-evaluation.

Business and industry should

- Realize the power they have to motivate and energize many learners by connecting the world of work with the curriculum.
- Recognize their responsibility to look for ways in which they can harness their resources to enhance the capacity of schools to meet learner needs.
- Understand that the most effective contribution they can make to the system, and therefore to their future workforce, is to work in partnership with education practitioners to devise structured, innovative approaches to meeting the needs of different groups of learners.
- Work to build local and national networks of businesses who are committed to playing their part in system transformation.

Local authorities should

- Work with each of the system components to create a shared vision for personalized learning across the local area.
- Use their resources effectively to harness the energy and expertise of all partners to implement the vision by brokering effective networks.
- Use local and national data to identify where there is successful practice relating to particular groups of learners and use resources to illuminate and understand why those successes are occurring.
- Develop effective strategies to disseminate successful practice and use resources to support schools in replicating that practice.
- Construct strategies to generate an understanding of what students feel about the quality of education provision locally.

References and acknowledgements

CBI (2005) *Employment Trends Survey*, CBI

Department for Skills and Education (1997) *Excellence in Schools*, DfES

Department for Skills and Education (1999) *Excellence in Cities*, DfES

Department for Skills and Education (2002) Roberts Review: *SET for Success – the supply of people with science, technology, engineering and mathematics skills*, DfES

Department for Skills and Education (2004a) *Every Child Matters*, DfES

Department for Skills and Education (2004b) *Five Year Strategy for Children and Learners*, DfES

Department for Skills and Education (2005a) *Higher Standards, Better Schools for All*, DfES

Department for Skills and Education (2005b) *Prospectus for High Performing Secondary Schools*, DfES

DfES, NCSL, IU and IDEA (2005) *Spreading Innovation Across Local Authorities: realising the potential of school-based networks*, DfES

Hull Lifelong Learning Partnership (2005) www.citylearning.net/reports

Miliband, David (2004) speech given at North of England Education Conference

The National Collaborative of Leading Edge Partnership Schools, NESTA (2006) motivation statements

The following figures have been supplied or redrawn – from DfES material: 2.1, 2.2, 2.3, 2.4, 2.5, 2.6 and 2.7; and 4.1 from Innovation Unit (2005) *Leading Edge Partnership Programme*, DfES; 5.1, 5.2 and Table 5.1 Fischer Family Trust, 2005

The authors would like to thank the following for permission to include details of innovation:

Bassingbourn Village College Partnership, Cambridgeshire

Dream Ireland

Fernwood Partnership, Nottingham

Haybridge High School Partnership

Park House School & Sports College, Berkshire

Penair School Partnership, Cornwall

Preston Manor, Alperton, Copland and Queens Park schools, Brent, London

St Thomas More Roman Catholic High School and Norham Community Technology College, Tyneside

The Thomas Hardye School, Dorchester

Valentines High School Partnership, Redbridge, Greater London

Index

accountability 5, 7–8, 9, 53
advice and guidance 8, 25
attainment 5, 6, 11–13
  and accountability 8
  case studies 15–17
  English 11f, 12f, 20
  and ethnicity 5, 14, 14f, 15–16, 17, 27, 31
  and gender 14f, 31
  government policy 9, 29
  impact on earning capacity 13, 13f
  Key Stage 2 11, 11f, 13
  Key Stage 3 11, 12f, 46
  Key Stage 4 12, 12f, 13, 13f, 18f, 20
  maths 11f, 12f, 20
  science 12f, 21
  sharing success 29–30
  and social class 5, 13f, 14–17, 14f, 18f, 27
  tests reliability and validity 12
attitudes to learning 17, 18–20

Barber, Michael 26, 27
Bassingbourn Village College Partnership 31
Beacon Schools 6
Blaze Radio 15
business and industry 43–7
  capacity 44
  innovative practice 44–7, 46t, 54
  key expectations 54
  needs 5, 20
  old model 43
  relationship and responsibilities 8, 43, 53, 54

capacity 34, 36, 44, 51
case studies 15–17
choice 8, 24–5
Clarke, Charles 24
collaboration *see* partnership and collaboration
Community Cohesion Standards 14
Confederation of British Industry (CBI) 20
curriculum 5–6, 8, 25, 26, 31, 53

data 37–41
  action research model 38–41, 39f, 40t
  asking the right questions 6, 38
  context and personalization 37–8
  for effective practice 30, 54
  examples of use 41
  government role 41, 53
  local authority role 54
  purpose 37
  sharing 30, 33, 50
Department for Skills and Education (DfES) 26
  accountability 7, 9, 53
  Innovation Unit 15, 38
  policy 14, 24, 27
diversity 8–9, 24–5, 53
drama 15–16
Dream Ireland 44–5

Education Action Zones 6
education system 7
English 11f, 12f, 20
  see also literacy
equity 24
ethnicity
  and attainment 5, 14, 14f, 15–16, 17, 27, 31
  case studies 15–17
  and peer mentoring 16–17
ethos 33
Every Child Matters 8, 24
Excellence in Cities 6

Fernwood Partnership 31
Films for Learning 45–6
Fischer Family Trust (FFT) 38–9
Five Year Strategy for Children and Learners 8–9, 24–5, 49
flexibility 24–5
the 'front line' 9
funding 8, 15, 25, 27, 50

gender 14f, 31
gifted and talented provision 27
government policy 23–7
  accountability 9
  attainment 9, 29
  data 41, 53
  diversity 8–9, 24–5

equity and choice 24
informed professionalism 26–7, 26f
initiatives and programmes 6, 8–9
key expectations 53
partnership and collaboration 27, 29–30
personalization 24, 27, 53
prescription 26
provision 23
public service delivery 23–4
standards 8, 23, 25, 27

Haybridge High School Partnership 31
Higher Education Funding Council for England (HEFCE) 21
Higher Standards, Better Schools for All 9, 24, 27
Hull Lifelong Learning Partnership 20

inclusion 6
informed professionalism 26–7, 26f
inspection 25

Jones, Sir Digby 20

key expectations 7, 10, 53–4
Key Stage 2 attainment 11, 11f, 13
Key Stage 3
   attainment 11, 12f, 46
   curriculum 25
   Strategy 9
Key Stage 4
   attainment 12, 12f, 13, 13f, 18f, 20
   curriculum 8, 25, 31

Leadership Incentive Grant Collaboratives 6, 29
Leading Edge Partnership Programme 34–5, 38–9
learning development officers 30
learning outcomes 15–16, 17, 54
learning styles 17, 19, 30, 34, 54
literacy 13, 14, 26, 27, 29, 43
   see also English
local authorities 49–51
   accountability 7, 8
   attitudinal surveys 20
   data use 54
   key challenges 50–1
   key expectations 54
   role 49
   services for personalization 50–1
   shared vision 49, 50, 53, 54

The Manor 15
maths 11f, 12f, 13, 14, 20, 21
   see also numeracy
modern foreign languages 20, 31
motivation 19, 20, 27, 31, 44, 46

National Collaborative 19, 46–7, 46t
National College of School Leadership (NCSL) 7–8
National Curriculum 26
National Foundation for Educational Research (NFER) 18
National Strategy consultants 9
National Youth Theatre 15
needs
   business and industry 5, 20
   students 5, 24, 27, 30, 33, 53
Network Learning Communities 29
Norham Community Technology College 41
numeracy 13, 26, 27, 29, 43
   see also maths

Ofsted 7, 25

Park House School & Sports College 19, 41
partnership and collaboration 7, 27, 29–36
   barriers 35–6
   capacity 34, 36
   from competition to collaboration 30
   data use 30, 33, 50
   establishing culture 33
   evaluation 32
   examples 31
   government policy 27, 29–30
   identifying areas for collaboration 34
   key premises 33
   levers for success 35–6
   offer to students 34
   practice model 33–6, 33f
   prioritizing 36
   self-evaluation 34–5
   sharing expertise 25, 30–1, 36
   systems and structures 32, 32f
   time 32, 35, 36
peer mentoring 16–17
Penair School Partnership 31
Performance Collaboratives 29
personalizing learning
   aim 7
   concept 5
   context 5–10

curriculum 5
  government policy 24, 27, 53
PHSE and Citizenship 15–16
Preston Manor School 15–16
professionalism 26–7, 26f, 33
provision 23
public service delivery 23–4

Roberts Review 21

school improvement 9
schools
  accountability 7
  key expectations 53–4
science 5, 12f, 14, 21, 31, 46–7
secondary education 6, 8–9, 24, 27
  see also Key Stage 3; Key Stage 4
self-esteem 15, 16–17, 19
self-evaluation 34–5
skills 20, 43
Smith, Jacqui 27
social class 5, 13f, 14–17, 14f, 18f, 27
special education needs 27
specialist schools 25, 27
Spreading Information Across Local Authorities 50–1

St Thomas More Roman Catholic High School 41
staff development 30, 34
  see also partnership and collaboration
stakeholders 43, 49, 50
standards 8, 23, 25, 27, 50
student voice 15, 17, 18–19, 24, 54
students' needs 5, 24, 27, 30, 33, 53
subject-specific issues 21
support 8, 9, 25

teaching and learning 5–6
technology 44–7
The Thomas Hardye School 41, 45–6
Training and Development Agency for Schools (TDA) 7–8
transition to secondary school 24
truancy 20

Valentines High School 15, 16–17
Valentines Partnership 31
vision 49, 50, 53, 54
vocational education 8, 25, 31

Young Apprenticeships 8

Other titles from Network Continuum Education

ACCELERATED LEARNING SERIES
Accelerated Learning: A User's Guide by Alistair Smith, Mark Lovatt & Derek Wise
Accelerated Learning in the Classroom by Alistair Smith
Accelerated Learning in Practice by Alistair Smith
The ALPS Approach: Accelerated learning in primary schools by Alistair Smith & Nicola Call
The ALPS Approach Resource Book by Alistair Smith & Nicola Call
MapWise by Oliver Caviglioli & Ian Harris
Creating an Accelerated Learning School by Mark Lovatt & Derek Wise
Thinking for Learning by Mel Rockett & Simon Percival
Reaching out to all learners by Cheshire LEA
Move It: Physical movement and learning by Alistair Smith
Coaching Solutions by Will Thomas & Alistair Smith
Coaching Solutions Resource Book by Will Thomas

ABLE AND TALENTED CHILDREN COLLECTION
Effective Provision for Able and Talented Children by Barry Teare
Effective Resources for Able and Talented Children by Barry Teare
More Effective Resources for Able and Talented Children by Barry Teare
Challenging Resources for Able and Talented Children by Barry Teare
Enrichment Activities for Able and Talented Children by Barry Teare
Problem Solving and Thinking Skills Resources for Able and Talented Children by Barry Teare
Parents' and Carers' Guide for Able and Talented Children by Barry Teare

LEARNING TO LEARN
The Practical Guide to Revision Techniques by Simon Percival
Let's Learn How to Learn: Workshops for Key Stage 2 by UFA National Team
Brain Friendly Revision by UFA National Team
Learning to Learn for Life: Research and practical examples for Foundation Stage and Key Stage 1 by Rebecca Goodbourn, Susie Parsons, Julia Wright, Steve Higgins & Kate Wall
Creating a Learning to Learn School by Toby Greany & Jill Rodd
Teaching Pupils How to Learn by Bill Lucas, Toby Greany, Jill Rodd & Ray Wicks

EXCITING ICT
New Tools for Learning: Accelerated learning meets ICT by John Davitt
Creative ICT in the Classroom: Using new tools for learning by the Learning Discovery Centre Team
Exciting ICT in Maths by Alison Clark-Jeavons
Exciting ICT in English by Tony Archdeacon
Exciting ICT in History by Ben Walsh
Exciting ICT in Science by Fergus Hegarty & Ken Brechin

PRIMARY RESOURCES
Foundations of Literacy by Sue Palmer & Ros Bayley
Flying Start with Literacy by Ros Bayley
The Thinking Child by Nicola Call with Sally Featherstone
The Thinking Child Resource Book by Nicola Call with Sally Featherstone
One Step at a Time by Ann Locke with Don Locke

Critical Skills in the Early Years by Vicki Charlesworth
Towards Successful Learning by Diana Pardoe
But Why? Developing philosophical thinking in the classroom by Sara Stanley with Steve Bowkett
Help Your Child To Succeed by Bill Lucas & Alistair Smith
Help Your Child To Succeed – Toolkit by Bill Lucas & Alistair Smith
Promoting Children's Well-Being in the Primary Years:
    The Right from the Start handbook edited by Andrew Burrell & Jeni Riley
Numeracy Activities Key Stage 2 by Afzal Ahmed & Honor Williams
Numeracy Activities Key Stage 3 by Afzal Ahmed, Honor Williams & George Wickham

LEARNING THROUGH SONGS

That's English! Learning English through songs (Key Stage 2) by Tim Harding
That's Maths! Learning maths through songs (Key Stage 2) by Tim Harding
Maths in Action! Learning maths through music & animation – interactive CD-ROM
    (Key Stage 2) by Tim Harding
That's Science! Learning science through songs (Key Stage 2) by Tim Harding
This is Science! Learning science through songs and stories (Key Stage 1) by Tim Harding

VISUAL LEARNING

Seeing History: Visual learning strategies & resources for Key Stage 3 by Tom Haward
Reaching out to all thinkers by Ian Harris & Oliver Caviglioli
Think it–Map it! by Ian Harris & Oliver Caviglioli
Thinking Skills & Eye Q by Oliver Caviglioli, Ian Harris & Bill Tindall

DISPLAY MATERIAL

Bright Sparks by Alistair Smith
More Bright Sparks by Alistair Smith
Leading Learning by Alistair Smith
Move It Posters: Physical movement and learning by Alistair Smith
Multiple Intelligence Posters (KS1 and KS2–4) edited by Alistair Smith
Emotional Intelligence Posters (KS1 and KS2–4) edited by Alistair Smith
Thinking Skills & Eye Q Posters by Oliver Caviglioli, Ian Harris & Bill Tindall

EMOTIONAL INTELLIGENCE

Multiple Intelligences in Practice: Enhancing self-esteem and learning in the classroom
    by Mike Fleetham
Moving to Secondary School by Lynda Measor with Mike Fleetham
Future Directions by Diane Carrington and Helen Whitten
Tooncards: A multi-purpose resource for developing communication skills by Chris Terrell
Becoming Emotionally Intelligent by Catherine Corrie
Lend Us Your Ears by Rosemary Sage
Class Talk by Rosemary Sage
A World of Difference by Rosemary Sage
Challenging Behaviour by Anne Copley
Best behaviour and Best behaviour FIRST AID by Peter Relf, Rod Hirst, Jan Richardson & Georgina Youdell
Self-Intelligence by Stephen Bowkett
Imagine That... by Stephen Bowkett
ALPS StoryMaker by Stephen Bowkett
StoryMaker Catch Pack by Stephen Bowkett
With Drama in Mind by Patrice Baldwin

PERSONALIZING LEARNING

Personalizing Learning: Transforming education for every child by John West-Burnham & Max Coates
Transforming Education for Every Child: A practical handbook by John West-Burnham & Max Coates
Personalizing Learning: How to Transform Learning through System-Wide Reform by Phil Jones & Maureen Burns
Personalizing Learning in the 21st Century edited by Sara de Freitas & Chris Yapp
The Power of Diversity by Barbara Prashnig
Learning Styles in Action by Barbara Prashnig

EFFECTIVE LEARNING & LEADERSHIP

Effective Heads of Department by Phil Jones & Nick Sparks
Leading the Learning School by Colin Weatherley
Transforming Teaching & Learning by Colin Weatherley with Bruce Bonney, John Kerr & Jo Morrison
Classroom Management by Philip Waterhouse & Chris Dickinson
Effective Learning Activities by Chris Dickinson
Making Pupil Data Powerful by Maggie Pringle & Tony Cobb
Raising Boys' Achievement by Jon Pickering
Getting Started by Henry Liebling
Closing the Learning Gap by Mike Hughes
Strategies for Closing the Learning Gap by Mike Hughes with Andy Vass
Tweak to Transform by Mike Hughes
Lessons are for Learning by Mike Hughes
Nurturing Independent Thinkers edited by Mike Bosher & Patrick Hazlewood
Effective Teachers by Tony Swainston
Effective Teachers in Primary Schools by Tony Swainston
Effective Leadership in Schools by Tony Swainston
Leading Change in Schools: A Practical Handbook by Sian Case
Learn to Transform by David Crossley with Graham Corbyn

VISIONS OF EDUCATION SERIES

Discover Your Hidden Talents: The essential guide to lifelong learning by Bill Lucas
The Brain's Behind It by Alistair Smith
Wise Up by Guy Claxton
The Unfinished Revolution by John Abbott & Terry Ryan
The Learning Revolution by Gordon Dryden & Jeannette Vos

SCHOOL GOVERNORS

Questions School Governors Ask by Joan Sallis
Basics for School Governors by Joan Sallis
The Effective School Governor by David Marriott (including audio tape)

For more information and ordering details, please consult our website
www.networkcontinuum.co.uk

Network Continuum Education – much more than publishing...

Network Continuum Education Conferences – Invigorate your teaching

Each term NCE runs a wide range of conferences on cutting edge issues in teaching and learning at venues around the UK. The emphasis is always highly practical. Regular presenters include some of our top-selling authors such as Sue Palmer, Mike Hughes and Steve Bowkett. Dates and venues for our current programme of conferences can be found on our website www.networkcontinuum.co.uk.

NCE online Learning Style Analysis – Find out how your students prefer to learn

Discovering what makes your students tick is the key to personalizing learning. NCE's Learning Style Analysis is a 50-question online evaluation that can give an immediate and thorough learning profile for every student in your class. It reveals how, when and where they learn best, whether they are right brain or left brain dominant, analytic or holistic, whether they are strongly auditory, visual, kinesthetic or tactile... and a great deal more. And for teachers who'd like to take the next step, LSA enables you to create a whole-class profile for precision lesson planning.

Developed by The Creative Learning Company in New Zealand and based on the work of Learning Styles expert Barbara Prashnig, this powerful tool allows you to analyse your own and your students' learning preferences in a more detailed way than any other product we have ever seen. To find out more about Learning Style Analysis or to order profiles visit www.networkcontinuum.co.uk/lsa.

Also available: Teaching Style Analysis and Working Style Analysis.

NCE's Critical Skills Programme – Teach your students skills for lifelong learning

The Critical Skills Programme puts pupils at the heart of learning, by providing the skills required to be successful in school and life. Classrooms are developed into effective learning environments, where pupils work collaboratively and feel safe enough to take 'learning risks'. Pupils have more ownership of their learning across the whole curriculum and are encouraged to develop not only subject knowledge but the fundamental skills of:

- problem solving
- creative thinking
- decision making
- communication
- management
- organization
- leadership
- self-direction
- quality working
- collaboration
- enterprise
- community involvement

'The Critical Skills Programme... energizes students to think in an enterprising way. CSP gets students to think for themselves, solve problems in teams, think outside the box, to work in a structured manner. CSP is the ideal way to forge an enterprising student culture.'

Rick Lee, Deputy Director, Barrow Community Learning Partnership

To find out more about CSP training visit the Critical Skills Programme website at www.criticalskills.co.uk